Royal Academy of Dancing

STEP · BY · STEP

BALLET
CLASS

D1305732

Royal Academy of Dancing

STEP · BY · STEP

BALLET
CLASS

*An illustrated
guide to the
official ballet
syllabus*

EBURY PRESS
LONDON

First published in 1993
Paperback edition published in 1998

3 5 7 9 10 8 6 4

Text copyright © Royal Academy of Dancing 1993
Illustrations copyright © Ebury Press 1993

First published in the United Kingdom in 1993 by
Ebury Press
Random House, 20 Vauxhall Bridge Road, London SW1V 2SA

Random House Australia (Pty) Limited
20 Alfred Street, Milsons Point, Sydney,
New South Wales 2061, Australia

Random House New Zealand Limited
18 Poland Road, Glenfield,
Auckland 10, New Zealand

Random House South Africa (Pty) Limited
Endulini, 5a Jubilee Road, Parktown 2193, South Africa

Random House UK Limited Reg. No. 954009

A CIP catalogue record for this book is
available from the British Library

ILLUSTRATIONS: BIZ HULL
Editor: Jane Struthers
Design: Roger Daniels

ISBN 0 09 186531 X

Typeset by SX Composing Ltd, Rayleigh, Essex
Printed and bound in Great Britain by
Butler & Tanner Ltd, Frome and London

Papers used by Ebury Press are natural recyclable
products made from wood grown in sustainable forests

ACKNOWLEDGEMENTS

The Royal Academy of Dancing would like to thank
Susan Danby LRAD ARAD, Principal of the College, for
writing and co-ordinating the text, with acknowledgements
to the following for their contribution:

David Watchman
Chief Executive
John Byrne ARAD (Dip PDTC)
Artistic Director
Valerie Hitchen Dip RBS (TTC)
Jane Pledger
Brenda Taylor

CONTENTS

─────KEY EXERCISES FROM THE GRADES─────

FOREWORD
BY ANTOINETTE SIBLEY

I FOUND THIS CHARMING BOOK, with its clear illustrations, lovely photographs and wise words helpful, interesting and enjoyable. It is not intended to teach pupils how to dance, but is meant as an additional and very useful guide to their study. It will add to their knowledge of ballet technique and at the same time open up the fascinating world of the dance.

There were three things that initially attracted, then bewitched, and finally held me captive in the ballet firmament. First, the sheer joy of moving to music; then the fascination with interpreting it and, last but not least, the lure of that special world of make-believe, the stage. But then there is an extra bonus for a ballet student. It is actually *good* for you, to dance. It is a healthy occupation, good for the body physically, teaching deportment and control of the limbs, and also good for the mind, teaching discipline, which will last a lifetime.

It is important for you, the pupil, to follow the guidelines set by your teacher and also by this book. You must make progress slowly, so you don't overstretch yourself, since this can cause problems in the future. Examinations are important as well. It is very useful to have someone, other than your own teacher, assessing your progress; and remember that your examiners will be of national and international repute, so your results will be of real value.

Some of you will want to go on to teach or become examiners. Others will want to perform on stage or, maybe, enjoy being spectators. Everyone will be helped by this delightful book and perhaps even your teachers will find themselves dipping into it to jog their own memories!

ANTOINETTE SIBLEY
President of the R.A.D.

How to Find a Ballet School

WHEN ANTOINETTE SIBLEY, the President of the Royal Academy of Dancing, first went to dancing class she was fortunate, for not only had her family been evacuated from London to Shrewsbury during the Second World War but so had the Cone-Ripman School. This was a dancing school of repute, offering not only ballet but modern theatre dance, national and tap, all essential elements of any dancer's training. When the war was over Antoinette Sibley followed the Cone-Ripmans to Tring Park, where the school became known as the Arts Educational School. Then, at the age of ten, she was accepted into the Royal Ballet School.

Never take a chance when looking for a school and a teacher. At worst, actual physical damage can result from bad teaching, at best young dancers with potential will become bored and want to give up. Sadly, even now, after years of experience, there are still teachers who ignore boys, or allow girls to dance on *pointe* years too early, ruining their feet.

If you want to be sure a dancing school is reputable, you can obtain a booklet of registered teachers from one of the big teaching and examining organizations, such as the Royal Academy of Dancing or the Imperial Society of Teachers of Dancing. In these booklets, the teachers' experience and qualifications are listed and the advantage to you is that the standard and good practice of these teachers is regularly monitored by the organization concerned. Nevertheless, it is still worthwhile taking the precaution of watching a class, to be sure that this is the right school for you. Most reputable schools will be more than happy to let you see a class of the right level and age group and there may be an opportunity to view the school performance or demonstration where you can judge for yourself the overall standard, as well as the general appearance of the pupils. It is important that they look happy and relaxed when performing. Other sources of useful information can be found in such magazines as *The Dancing Times* in Britain, *Dance Magazine* in America and *Dance Australia* in Australia – or, indeed, in Yellow Pages!

If you are able to see a class you should note what the room is like as well as the teaching standard. A good non-slip floor is essential and the studio should be light and airy. The number of pupils in the class should ideally be around 15 to 20. If pupils are packed in they have neither the room to move nor the chance of sufficient individual attention from the teacher.

The grooming and appearance of the teacher is just as important as that of the pupils, as they are bound to be influenced by him or her. Watch keenly for how much individual care children get and how much sympathetic correction. Too many teachers set a step or *enchaînement* and then just sit back and watch it. Too much correction can be bad in the early years when pupils should dance largely for fun and to build up stamina and rhythmic ability, but the time soon comes when the poise of the head, the placing of the body and the pointing of the feet are absolutely essential and should constantly be watched for by the teacher.

For many years ballet classes were accompanied by very uninspiring music. But nowadays, teachers are much more likely to use music which is of the correct tempo, and with which children can identify and enjoy dancing to. Musical appreciation should be a part of the training, and classes should not be regimented to strict tempo music. Live music is invariably best, but there may be difficulties in arranging it. Many good quality tapes are made specially for class by leading ballet pianists and teachers.

Having chosen a school it is difficult to know exactly how much you should be paying. As with many purchases the most expensive is not necessarily best, nor will the cheapest always be the worst. The extra money may go towards unnecessary facilities while the cheapest school may have the most talented teacher. This has to be a matter of personal judgement.

Your Ballet Class

As a young girl, Margot Fonteyn one day saw a poster of a ballerina and asked her mother who it was. 'That's Pavlova, the greatest dancer in the world', her mother told her. 'Then I will be the second greatest', she replied.

All dancers need this confidence, though they may not all grow up to be a Prima Ballerina Assoluta! Nevertheless, even though they may know they will never make it to the very top many dancers feel they have achieved their life's ambition through dancing. Ballet is exhausting and time-consuming, but it is also exciting and creative and many dancers become totally dedicated to their profession. It is a whole world of its own.

The professional dancer's life needs a lot of self-discipline, so it is important that you learn to be independent early on. For example, try to look after your own practice clothes yourself, and make sure they are always clean and in good repair – don't leave them for someone else to deal with. Give yourself a brief moment to relax and put yourself in the right frame of mind before you begin class. Doing these things for yourself will help you to feel more confident and self-assured.

Once class has started, listen carefully and try to keep your mind on what you are being asked to do. When you first begin ballet you may find this difficult, as many of the seemingly simple movements need to be repeated very often to get them right. A good teacher will know how to keep your interest, occasionally re-arranging your syllabus steps and allowing you to relax and have fun for a while.

Your teacher is there to guide and assist you through difficult moments, but there are many ways in which you can help yourself in this respect. For instance, don't be tempted to chat to your neighbour, for that means you are not listening to your teacher and are also disturbing someone else's concentration. Your teacher will correct your movements from time to time. Try to understand why and work hard to get them right. Pay attention to other pupils' corrections because they might apply to you, too!

There is no better way of learning to dance than studying with other people who are equally interested and motivated to succeed. Learning in this way, you can judge your own progress and can compare yourself with others. If you have a particular fault which needs correcting, your teacher may think it is a good idea to have private lessons. On the whole, though, learning in class is better, as private lessons tend to concentrate on what has not been achieved rather than on what has – in other words, your bad points rather than your good points, which may make you feel rather pessimistic about your chances of succeeding. Although it requires tremendous effort, your ballet class should also be *fun* and something to be looked forward to. How much you enjoy it can be greatly helped by interesting accompanying music. Listen to the music, for it will affect how you express yourself in movement. After all, dance is an art.

Sometimes, you may feel that you are not progressing quickly enough, but be patient and trust your teacher. Years of experience will have taught him or her to look at your development and to decide on the right pace for you. Doing too much too early can be more damaging than being held back a little.

A little discomfort is to be expected in a ballet class, but do not push yourself too hard for, however carefully you are taught, accidents can happen. If you are in real pain, tell your teacher at once and act on his or her advice.

Working in a disciplined way will not only help you to achieve much in your dancing; it should also assist you in other areas of study – and generally prepare you for life in the future. Ask any professional dancer and he or she will tell you that good concentration and a sense of self-discipline are absolutely essential qualities if you are intending to take up dancing seriously. Nevertheless, have fun!

Dressing for Dance

LIKE MANY OTHER PROFESSIONS, dance has a uniform of its own. Very young dancers, just taking their first steps and learning to enjoy movement, should wear comfortable, almost everyday clothes: full skirts for girls and shorts for boys. As they develop they will need to dispense with these, wearing just a close-fitting leotard and tights (or socks) to give the necessary freedom of movement. The leotard has been accepted practice costume for dancers since Monsieur Leotard invented it in France over a hundred years ago.

How to Choose a Leotard

The correct measurement is essential and should be done in a specialist shop by an experienced assistant. If you wish to take the measurement yourself you must measure the exact girth by placing the end of a tape measure on one shoulder, bringing it down the front of the body, between the legs, and back up to the same shoulder. This gives you the correct size of leotard to buy. A leotard which is too small will be uncomfortable and will restrict movement, but even more importantly, if it is too large the outline of the body will be obscured and the teacher may miss faults in placing and movement. It is very tempting to buy a leotard with growing room, but it is a temptation which should be resisted.

Where to Buy Shoes and How to Fit Them

Some local shoe shops stock ballet shoes, but it is best to go to one of the specialist dance shops. As ballet shoes are designed to fit like a second skin it is essential that they are fitted properly and, once again, that you should *not* allow any growing room. Girls' shoes are made of satin or kid leather and are held on with elastic, satin or nylon ribbons. Boys' shoes are made of kid leather or canvas and held on with narrow elastic which should not be too tight. The illustrations below show where to attach the ribbon (which comes in one length and must be cut into four equal parts) or elastic, and how to tie them neatly so that there

are no untidy bows or loose ends, which not only get in the way of working efficiently but also look ugly and ruin the line of a stretched foot.

Kind relatives are often tempted to buy ballet shoes, particularly satin ones, as presents, but it would be better if they sent the money instead. Fitting your shoes needs expert guidance, and mistakes made early on can cause problems in the future. This is even more important when girls progress to *pointe* work, around the age of 11. Finding the right *pointe* shoes can be a very difficult business and may take visits to more than one specialist manufacturer. It may even be necessary to have your shoes specially made. The cost of this service is not as great as you might think, as the *pointe* shoe industry is used to dealing with every known shape and size of foot.

Though it is unwise to wear second-hand shoes as a way of keeping down the cost of ballet training, well organized schools may arrange for sales of good quality second-hand uniforms. It is, of course, possible to make simple skirts yourself, and if you enjoy knitting there is plenty of scope for making your own leg-warmers!

As the origin of theatrical Character dance lies in its folk counterpart, special shoes, heavier and with a heel, will be needed for this section of the class. Though these shoes are more akin to an ordinary outdoor shoe, they will still need to be fitted properly if your feet are not to appear clumsy and awkward as you dance. Girls will also need a Character skirt made of heavy cotton. One cut in a full circle gives the most movement and is more flattering to the figure than a gathered skirt. It should be attached to a waistband and reach approximately mid-calf, though on some girls it may need to be a little shorter or a little longer to keep the body overall in proportion. Brightly coloured ribbons may be sewn near the hem.

General Grooming

Every dance-wear shop now stocks a fantastic range of brightly coloured dance clothes, striped leg-warmers and jazzy leotards. Fun though

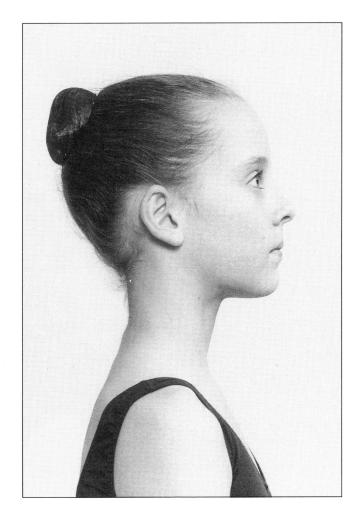

these may be, they are not for the young ballet student. With them the dance class becomes a show, and the leg-warmers hide badly pointed feet from the teacher's eye!

Fortunately, most schools follow the guidelines set up by the examining organizations and insist on a simple basic uniform, though nowadays there is much more variety than there has been in the past.

A dancer should always be perfectly dressed and groomed. It is part of the self-discipline which goes hand-in-hand with the ballet training itself, and is evidence of the pupil's serious approach. The most obvious points to remember are that shoes should be neat and clean and the leotard should fit correctly and comfortably.

Boys should wear their hair short. Girls should choose a neat style with long hair tied back, preferably into a bun to give a good line to the head and neck. Long fringes should be pinned back to show the face clearly, and no jewellery should be worn during the class. It distracts the teacher's eye and if it flies off can prove dangerous to the others in the class.

R · E · M · E · M · B · E · R
To put the following in your dance bag each week:
1 Clean leotard.
2 Clean socks or tights.
3 Clean shoes.
4 All the things necessary to make your hair neat and tidy.
5 Any props needed for class or for the Character dance.

How to Tie the Ribbons

1 Cross the ribbons over in front of the ankle (satin ribbons have a special backing to prevent them from slipping).

2 Take the ribbons round behind the ankle and cross them over again.

3 Lie one on top of the other in front of the leg (not too high up).

4 Bring the ends round to the inside of the ankle and knot them tightly by the hollow next to the ankle bone.

5 To prevent the knot from slipping, wet it with a little water before tucking it, along with the ends, underneath the ribbons. The ribbon that you buy comes in a standard length. Cut the excess (approx 2.5cm/1in) off close to the knot in order to make a neat finish.

1

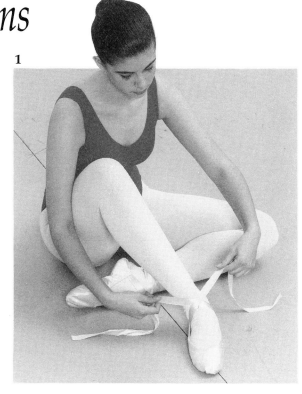

3

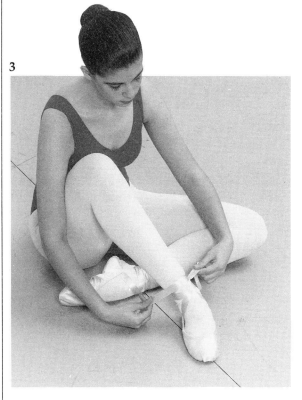

4

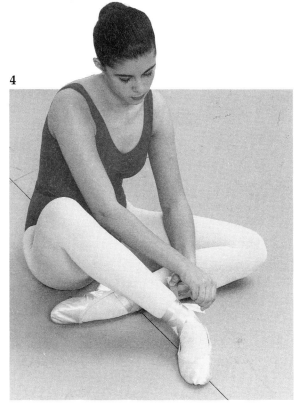

2

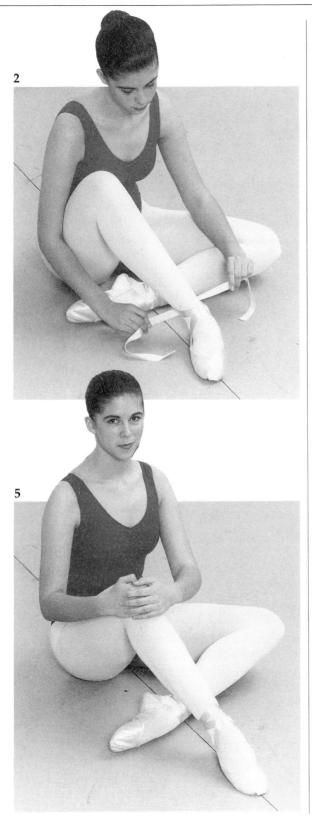

5

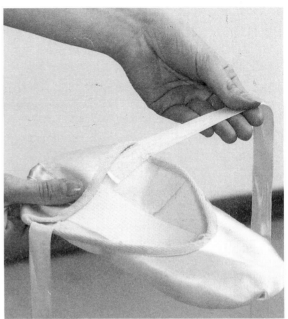

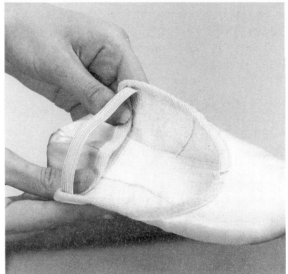

Bend the back of the shoe forwards against the insole. Attach the ribbon (top) or elastic (above) securely at the point of the fold, without sewing through the drawstring which runs round the upper edge of the shoe and which tightens this edge so that it lies close to the foot without gaping. The drawstring should be tied in a bow (not a knot as it may work loose from time to time) with the ends tucked in under the shoe.

Glossary of Terms

à la seconde To second position.

à terre On the ground.

adage The part of the class where slow, flowing, controlled movements are combined to develop grace, beauty and balance.

allegro The part of the class where small, big and travelling steps are demonstrated in varying speeds and rhythms.

arabesque A position in which the dancer balances on one leg with the other extended behind.

arrière (en) Backwards.

assemblé Assembled, or brought together.

avant (en) Forwards.

balancé *Balancer* means to swing or to rock.

barre A bar that you hold on to while doing the first part of your class (from Grade One onwards) to help you to develop strength and skill while being supported.

battement Literally translated, it means a beating movement.

battement frappé *Frappé* means 'struck' – the ball of the foot strikes the surface of the floor as the leg extends to an open position.

battement glissé *Glissé* means 'sliding' or 'gliding'. The foot slides out with enough energy to bring the toes just off the floor.

battement tendu *Tendu* means 'stretched'. The leg and foot are stretched away from the body – the toes remaining on the ground.

bourrée An eighteenth-century dance.

bras bas Arms down. This is a position of the arms from which all other positions commence. It is also a resting position for the arms.

changements Springs in which you change your feet in the air.

changer To change.

chasser To chase or hunt.

chassé Chased or hunted.

côté To the side or sideways.

cou-de-pied Neck of the foot, or ankle joint.

croisé (en) A direction of the body in which one side of the body is turned slightly away from the front, with the leg nearest the audience crossed in front of the other one.

coupé Cut, ie to cut the weight from one foot to the other, with or without a spring.

couper To cut.

danseur noble A dancer of fine appearance.

de côté To the side or moving sideways.

dedans (en) Inwards.

dégagé Means to 'free, separate, disengage'. The term given to the movement of the leg and foot when it is separated or disengaged from a closed to an open position *à terre*.

dehors (en) Outwards.

demi-bras Half-arms. A position of the arms, found halfway between the first and second positions, with the palms turned slightly upwards.

demi-pliés Half-bend.

demi-pointe Half-point, ie to stand on the ball of the foot.

demi-seconde Half-second. A position of the arms found halfway between second position and *bras bas*.

derrière Behind.

devant In front.

développé To open out, unfold, develop.

écarté (en) Separated, or thrown apart. One leg is stretched to second position with the body turned slightly away from the audience and head turned over the front shoulder.

echapper To escape.

echappé sauté A spring in which the feet escape from each other at the highest point and land in an open position.

en arrière Backwards.

en avant Forwards.

en croisé Crossed. One side of the body is turned away from the front with the leg nearest the audience crossed in front of the other one.

en croix In the shape of a cross.

en dedans Inwards.

en écarté See *écarté* above.
en face To the front, facing the front.
en fondu Melted, sunken, bent.
enchaînement *Enchaîner* means 'to link' and *enchaînement* is when two or more steps are linked together and danced to music.
en l'air In the air.
en ouvert Open or to the open direction.

face (en) Facing the front.
fondu (en) Melted, ie sinking gently down into a bend on one leg.
frappé Beaten or struck.
fouetté Whipped.
fouetter To whip.
full pointe Standing on the top of the toes in shoes specially made to protect the feet.

galop A travelling step, done sideways or forwards or around the outside of the room.
glissade A gliding step which serves as a preparation or as a link for others.
glissé Sliding or gliding.
grand, grande Big, large.
grand battement A movement taken at the *barre* and later in the centre in which the leg is thrown from the hip joint high into the air.
grand plié A bending of the knees in a *plié* until the thighs are horizontal with the floor.

jeter To throw.

l'air (en) In the air.

oblique (line, of arabesque) A slanting line.
ouvert (en) Open.

pas A step.
pas de basque Step from the Basque region.
pas de bourrée Step of the *bourrée*, an eighteenth-century dance.
pas de chat Step of a cat.
passé Passed.
passer To pass.
petit Little, small.

petits jetés Small springs from one leg to the other.
pirouette A turn or spin on one leg.
pirouette en dedans A *pirouette* turning inwards.
pirouette en dehors A *pirouette* turning outwards.
pirouette position The position in which you turn.
plié A bending of the knees.
plier To bend.
pointe, demi To stand on half point, ie on the ball of your foot.
pointe, full To stand on the top of your toes in shoes specially made to protect your feet.
ports de bras Carriage of the arms. There are *ports de bras* exercises in all grades to help you learn to move your arms gracefully and expressively.
poser To step out in any direction.

relevé Lifted or raised up.
retiré Withdrawn. A movement in which you draw up your thigh in second position, knee bent, sliding the toes up the side of the supporting leg until they reach the hollow at the back of the knee.
révérence A curtsey or bow.
ronds de jambe Circular movements of the leg.
rotation Rotation, usually of the thigh.

sauté sprung.
sauter To spring.
seconde, à la To second position.
soubresaut A spring from two feet to two feet without a change, crossing one leg in front of the other in the air, so the back foot is hidden by the front one.

temps levé To spring in the air from one leg.
tendu Stretched.
terre (à) On the ground.
tour en l'air A spring in which you make one or more turns in the air before landing.

Taking an Examination

IT IS NATURAL TO FEEL a little nervous before an exam. Margot Fonteyn always had a temperature for three days before her exams, causing her family a great deal of worry, but she always seemed to recover on the day to pass to everyone's satisfaction. If you are well prepared by your teacher for your exam you should look forward to it with excitement and anticipation.

You should remember that the examination is only a way of you and your teacher *together* seeing how you are progressing. The results are not necessarily an indication of whether or not you are going to become a professional dancer. They are just the first rungs of a very long ladder, and their aim is to set you on the upward path so you can continue to progress.

Your teacher will let you know when you are ready to take a particular exam, and it is likely that you will have had at least a year's study of a wider syllabus before you approach it, with a little extra work on the set syllabus for the exam nearer the date. Your teacher may even advise that you should take a few extra classes as the exam draws near. You can always do a little work at home by yourself but it is best to keep this to a minimum, perhaps just refreshing your memory about the French ballet terms so that when your examiner asks for a particular step or movement you will not have to think too hard and will therefore be more relaxed.

Your teacher will also help you to gain confidence by letting you know other details of what will be expected of you. As your teacher will have prepared many pupils for exams, he or she will let you know exactly how to enter and leave the examination room, and how to behave during the exam itself. Having a full knowledge of these important facts will help you feel more comfortable and confident.

If your examination is not taking place at your own school, your teacher will almost certainly arrange for you to take a look at the new room. Then you can check to see what the floor surface is like, or if the room is an unusual shape. Try your hand on the *barre* as it might be different in some way to the one you are used to, and also notice the lighting, which might distract you. All these points will help you feel absolutely comfortable, leaving you to put all your thought and energy into your dancing.

Having the right clothes and props is also important. When Margot Fonteyn arrived at Sadler's Wells Theatre for her first audition she did not take any practice clothes or ballet shoes, so she auditioned barefoot in her petticoat. She succeeded, but your examiner might not be so pleased with you if by any chance you did the same! Fortunately this is a worry you are unlikely to have as there will almost certainly be special rules about your uniform depending on your particular syllabus. Everyone will need his or her regular practice clothes and both boys and girls will need special shoes for the Character section: girls will also need a Character skirt. You might be tempted to keep a new pair of shoes or a new leotard specially for the day, but this can be unwise as you could feel very uncomfortable in them. If your syllabus requires that you should wear your hair in a particular style it is a good idea to try the style out a few times in advance to make sure you can put it up securely, especially if it is very different from your usual one. If you don't do this, you might find that your head movements feel strange or restricted on examination day.

As you can see, all this advice is to make you feel better on the day so that you can perform naturally and with confidence. Examiners are not there to frighten you, as they have a pretty good idea of how you are feeling, and will do their best to put you at your ease, particularly as you both have something in common – a love of dancing. It's worth remembering that they are just as likely to enjoy watching a relaxed and happy dancer who has a good sense of music and performance as they are a dancer who performs all the set steps perfectly, but without any show of feeling.

Key Exercises from the Grades

THE INTENTION of this part of the book is to show the progression from the Royal Academy of Dancing's Grades Pre-Primary to Grade Five for children and young students. It does not include the three final grades since these concern themselves not so much with new vocabulary but with style, in particular the style of the Romantic period in the nineteenth century from which classical ballet, as we know it today, evolved. The book is not a teaching manual, so only certain steps and movements have been shown, either because their progression is obvious or because they are well-known and can be identified in the current ballet repertoire. Each grade is written with the assumption that the reader has studied the previous grades so, whenever a step or movement is repeated, only the points relevant to that grade are mentioned to avoid too much repetition. The book also assumes the reader will browse through this part of the book while learning new steps with the teacher, to act as a reminder. Learning *only* from a book would be dull.

The exercises in this book are part of the RAD method for both boys and girls. Apart from the first two levels, all the ballet movements are given a French name, since French is the language used for ballet throughout the world.

Preliminary Positions and Posture

This chapter teaches you the basic positions of the body, arms and feet. As balletic movement connects one position to another, it is very important to remember them.

THE POSITIONS OF THE ARMS

Ports de Bras

When the arms move continuously through some of these positions, or other ones, it is called *ports de bras*. This actually means 'carriage of the arms', but to you it should suggest the way in which your arms move gracefully and expressively, in harmony with the rest of your body, when you are dancing. You will find *ports de bras* exercises in each grade from Primary onwards. They are specially designed to practise moving your arms through different positions and shapes and include the use of the legs and body in later grades.

The position of the arms from which all other positions start is called *bras bas*. In English it means 'arms down' and it also serves as a resting place in between exercises.

BRAS BAS
The arms, which are held a little in front of the body, should be relaxed and a little rounded at the elbow, with the fingers continuing the curve in the arm to create an oval shape. The little finger is closest to the leg.

From *bras bas* the five basic positions of the arms can be made.

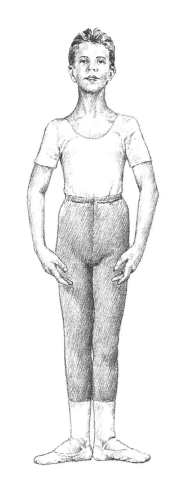

R · E · M · E · M · B · E · R

● Relax your shoulders.

● Keep your thumbs close to the other fingers.

● Try not to show the backs of your hands.

1st Position

This is a gateway to all the other positions. You almost always go through 1st position to get to any other position of the arms.

2nd Position

In this position there should be a slight slope downwards from your shoulders to your wrists – just enough to allow a small drop of water to trickle slowly down your arms.

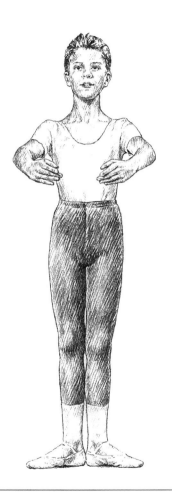

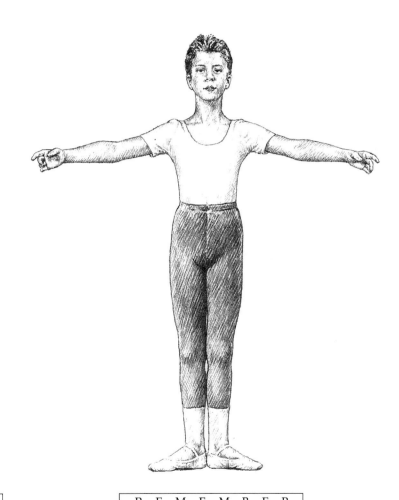

R · E · M · E · M · B · E · R
● Relax your shoulders.
● Support your elbows.
● Keep the palms of your hands facing you.

R · E · M · E · M · B · E · R
● Keep your shoulders relaxed.
● Keep your arms gently curved with the centre of your palms facing the front.
● Support your elbows.

THE POSITIONS OF THE ARMS

3RD POSITION
One arm is placed in 1st position and the other in 2nd position.

4TH POSITION
One arm is placed in 2nd position and the other is raised high, slightly in front of the head.

5TH POSITION
Both arms are raised high with the hands a little in front of the body.

R · E · M · E · M · B · E · R
• Not to over-cross the arm in front.
• All the points made regarding 1st and 2nd positions.

R · E · M · E · M · B · E · R
• Those shoulders!
• Check your posture – has it sagged anywhere?

R · E · M · E · M · B · E · R
• Keep your shoulders relaxed – they will be tempted to lift with your arms.
• Keep your palms towards you, not the audience.

DEMI-SECONDE

In addition to these basic positions there are two more which are useful for beginning or finishing exercises. The first is *demi-seconde*, which means 'half-second', and you will find it halfway between 2nd position and *bras bas*. The arms are held a little in front of the body.

DEMI-BRAS

The second is *demi-bras*, which means 'half-arms', and it is halfway between 1st and 2nd positions. In this position the hands open with the palms slightly upward as if you were asking for something (applause perhaps?) The arms are held lower than in 2nd position.

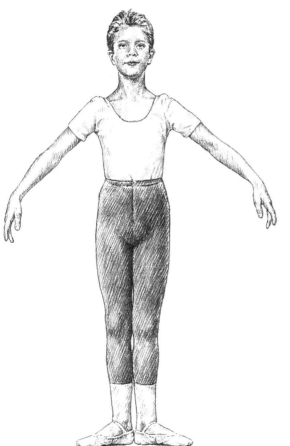

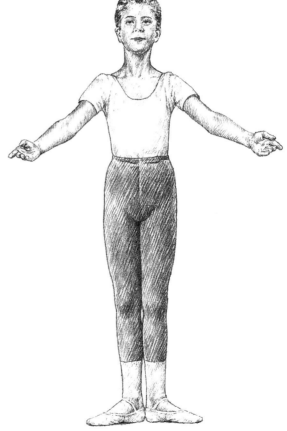

R · E · M · E · M · B · E · R

- Keep plenty of space and air between your upper arms and your sides.

- Keep the point of the elbow outwards to create a gentle arc to the fingertips.

R · E · M · E · M · B · E · R

- Keep the shoulders relaxed and open.

- Support the elbows.

- Place the hands at waist height – no higher!

THE POSITIONS OF THE FEET

The amount that you can turn your feet sideways in any position will depend on how much you can make your thigh turn outwards at the hip joint so that your knee is facing the same way as your foot. (The hip joint is where your leg is joined to your body.) Never push your foot out beyond the knee as this is cheating and it will cause problems later on.

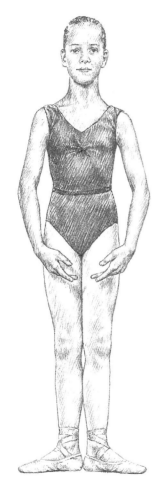

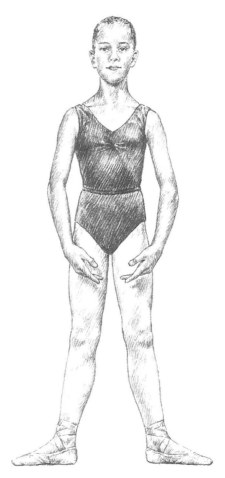

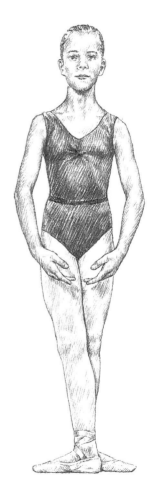

1ST POSITION
The heels are placed together with the toes pointed outwards and away from each other.

2ND POSITION
The distance between your feet should be approximately one-and-a-half times the length of your foot. Your teacher will help you to find the right position.

3RD POSITION
The heel of one foot is placed against the instep of the other.

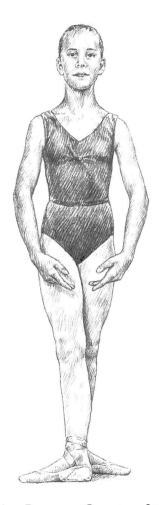

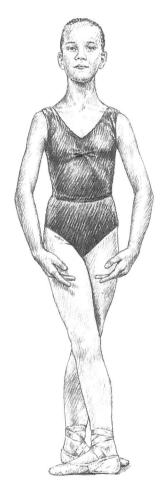

4TH POSITION OPPOSITE 3RD
One leg is taken forward with the heel of the front foot placed opposite the instep of the back foot (that is, opposite 3rd position). The weight is placed evenly between the feet and the distance between them is about the length of one of your feet.

4TH POSITION OPPOSITE 5TH
One leg is taken forward with the heel of the front foot placed opposite the toes of the back foot (that is, opposite 5th position). The weight distribution and the distance are the same as 4th opposite 3rd position.

5TH POSITION
The heel of one foot is placed beside the toe of the other. Your amount of turnout will depend, as always, upon what you can manage, but remember – it can be improved with practice!

GOOD POSTURE

Finally, before you read further, a dancer must always think about the way he or she is standing, for *nothing* will work correctly unless the body is held upright with the weight over the feet and without any sagging or arching in the spine (the bony column that runs up and down the back, on top of which the head is poised). It takes a long time to achieve this correct posture and so, although it will not always be mentioned in each exercise, you must think about it all the time during class or when you are practising alone.

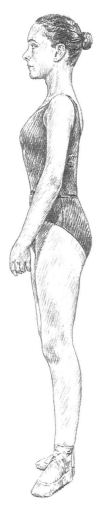

CORRECT POSTURE

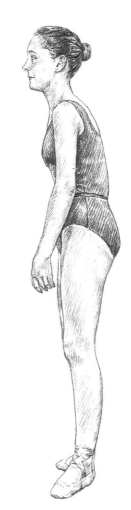

INCORRECT POSTURE
A sagging back

INCORRECT POSTURE
Arching the back

Pre-Primary Grade

At this stage you will learn to dance in many different ways, sometimes with a partner, as part of a group and sometimes on your own. It should be fun to do!

Exercise for Feet

This is one of the exercises you do sitting on the floor. Sit with your legs stretched out in front and your feet turned up, so your toes are pointing towards the ceiling. Your teacher may call them 'naughty toes' because they do not look at all like a dancer's feet! Help your back to stay straight by lightly placing your hands on either side of you on the floor. Now you are ready to begin. Gently stretch your feet, keeping the toes curled up. When your feet are pointing in the same direction as your legs, stretch out your toes too. Then quickly pull your toes back up and do the exercise again.

With straight knees, slowly push your feet away from you, toes curled up. Stretch your toes out last.

Demi-Pliés

This exercise, and the next one, are both technical rather than fun ones.

Demi-plié means 'half-bend' and is the first exercise to be called by its French name.

Point and Close

Start as you did for *demi-pliés*, with your heels touching and your toes apart. This is called 1st position of the feet because it is the first and easiest for you to learn. Have you got very tight knees to help you balance? If so, slide one leg forward until your foot is fully stretched. You learned how to do this in the first exercise. Lightly tap your stretched toes on the ground twice, before sliding your foot back home to join the other one. Now try with the other leg. Then do it all again.

Stand with your heels touching, toes slightly apart and with your body looking very straight and tall. Girls can put their hands on their waist like the boys or they can hold out the edge of their skirt slightly to make them feel more poised.

Bend your knees, opening them over your toes as if you were opening a window on either side.

Is there a big space and is your back tall and straight? Now stretch up, closing your knees tightly so there is no space left between them. Try doing this movement three times so you can begin to get used to it. Then have a short rest before you try again.

Try not to lift your heels off the floor when you bend your knees.

Slide your leg out in front of you and lightly tap the ground twice with your toes. Then bring your foot home to 1st position. Pull your tummy up tightly and keep the leg you are standing on straight, to help you balance while you are tapping. Then try with the other leg.

Walking with Stretched Feet

The last exercise will help you with this one, which comes from a part of the class where you move in a circle round the room. All dancers must learn how to walk with stretched feet because it makes their movements look much lighter.

Bounces

For bounces your feet are side by side, with your heels and toes together. Bounce up and down as high as you can, like a big rubber ball. Stretch your toes in the air and do not forget to bend your knees for a soft landing. Can you do 16 all in one go? Clap on the last bounce to remind yourself to stop.

Walk round the room putting your toes on the floor first instead of your heels. If you are a girl, hold the edges of your skirt. If you are a boy, clasp your hands behind your back – it will help to keep it well lifted.

Walk around the room placing your toes on the floor first. Remember to keep your back and head well lifted and listen carefully to the music.

Keeping your feet side by side, bounce up and down like a rubber ball. The more you stretch your legs and feet the higher you will go. Try to bounce in time with the music.

Pony Galops

For this exercise you will use a skipping rope. Towards the end of your class, you will do some dance steps which will include marching, pony trotting and joining simple steps together.

Galoping is fun because it can be done with a partner, in a group or by yourself with a skipping rope, which is how it is described here.

1 Start with your feet together and the skipping rope held low behind your legs, arms outstretched. Lift one foot up beside the knee of the other leg and begin to swing the rope forwards.

2 As the rope swings over your head hop into the air and begin to change over legs, letting the rope pass underneath them.

┌─────────────────────────────┐
│ R · E · M · E · M · B · E · R │
│   │
│ ● Keep the rope at arm's   │
│ length and work up a good   │
│ rhythm between rope, arms   │
│ and legs so you do not trip! │
└─────────────────────────────┘

3 Then step forward with the second leg and get ready to do it all over again.

Enchaînement

This *is* a long word and your teacher may call this exercise by a simpler name.

This is the last exercise you will learn in this grade. The word *enchaînement* means 'linking' and is the name given to two or more steps when they are linked together. An *enchaînement* can contain different directions of the body, floor patterns and arm and head movements, as well as positions and movements for the legs and feet. (In this grade it will be kept simple so you can work in a group.)

Later on, when all these things work in harmony with the music to produce a movement which flows from one position to another, it is called co-ordinated. At this stage, these *enchaînements* will be set by your teacher so you can practise making everything happen together, but later they may be free – that is, given by your teacher on the spur of the moment, to see if you have an alert brain and quick reactions.

Curtsey or Bow

At the end of the class your teacher will show you how to thank him or her and the pianist who may have come to play for you. It will be a curtsey or bow, depending on whether you are a girl or boy.

Primary Grade

Now it is time to learn to do everything with a little more care, but with just as much enjoyment. Like the previous grade, this one starts with exercises that you do sitting on the floor.

Exercise for Hands

You will already have been given exercises to make your hands and fingers expressive. Here is an exercise to make them look more delicate.

To start, either sit cross-legged or, if you find it more comfortable, kneel sitting back on your heels. Rest your hands on your knees.

1 Pick up your hands and gently bring your wrists together.

2 Beginning to stretch your fingers, squeeze the palms of your hands together until only the centres of your hands are touching.

3 Press your fingers together.

R · E · M · E · M · B · E · R
● Keep your elbows supported while you squeeze and peel your hands. It will make them work harder.
● Keep the movements simple, gentle and delicate.
● Watch them to make sure.

4 Now peel your fingers apart and open your hands gently, making a circular movement outwards and inwards, in order to join your wrists and start again from the beginning. Do this twice with two small circular movements outwards and once with a large one, this time taking longer to return to the starting position. This starting position looks like an exotic flower. Do you know which one?

Exercise for Legs

Sit as you did before, with your back lightly held by your arms and with your legs and feet stretched out in front (turn back in the book to remind yourself), but this time let your legs roll outwards so your knees are pointing away from each other. Now you are ready to begin.

> ### R·E·M·E·M·B·E·R
>
> ● Keep your legs well stretched as you roll them in and out.
>
> ● Hold your back and head well.
>
> ● As you lift your leg, look at your foot to see if it is still beautifully pointed.

1 Slowly roll your legs inwards until your knees are pointing up at the ceiling.

2 Roll them out. Do all that again, rolling your legs in and out.

3 Keeping your back straight, stretch one leg and foot away from you and lift it a little off the ground.

4 Lower the leg carefully to the floor. Try all that again from the beginning, lifting the other leg into the air next time.

31

Port de Bras

Do you remember what this means? In this grade, there are two *ports de bras*, one for using your hands and arms delicately, the other to show a stronger, firmer use of your arm.

Swaying

This comes from a part of your class called Free Movement, which will be described more fully in a later grade, but for now you should know that it allows you to move in a freer way than your classical ballet. It is the first time in this book that you are going to hold something in your hand to help you feel the movement correctly. You could hold a scarf if you are a girl or a flag if you are a boy.

1 Stand with your feet in 1st position (not too turned out) with the scarf or flag in your right hand. Take a good step to the side with your right foot, at the same time swinging your right arm out. Follow the scarf or flag with your eyes.

2 Sway back over your left leg, swinging your right arm across your body. Look at the scarf or flag. Do it several times until it feels easier.

Now try starting the exercise to the left, with the scarf or flag in your left hand.

Demi-pliés

Do you remember this exercise from Pre-Primary? In this grade it is practised in two positions, 2nd then 1st. There is one count to bend your knees and one to straighten them carefully and tightly. The movement will make the muscles in your legs stretch gently while you keep your balance over your feet. *Demi-plié* is very useful and important because many springing steps begin and end with it. You will come across it often from now on.

R · E · M · E · M · B · E · R
● Keep your knees out over your toes.
● Keep your back straight.
● It sounds easy but it isn't!

Walks and Point

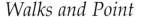

Do you remember Point and Close and Walking with Stretched Feet from Pre-Primary? In this grade you are going to put the two together. To make it a little harder, after three walks forward there will be only one point AND the leg you are standing on will be bent. Don't worry, you will have practised the hard part in a previous exercise! It can be done in a circle so you can keep practising it, or it can be done walking along a straight line from one corner of the room to the opposite one (this is called *en diagonale*).

Place your bent knee over your toes. Try to turn your stretched leg out so its knee is pointing away from the bent one. (Where did you learn to roll your leg outwards like that?)

1 Start with your feet in 2nd position and your hands on your waist, fingers together.

2 Bend your knees without raising your heels and with your body placed equally between your feet. Your knees are placed over your toes, with your back held upright and your head poised.

R · E · M · E · M · B · E · R
● Keep your head well poised, as if you were wearing a crown.
● Keep your back upright to match your head.
● Turn your foot out only as far as your knee can catch up with it!

Sautés

A *sauté* is a spring and it begins and ends in a *demi-plié*. Instead of just bouncing as you did in Pre-Primary, you are going to learn how to stretch your feet fully in the air and how to come down in 1st position, heels together, knees open and back held upright – *all without making a noise*. If this sounds difficult, it is! Look at it from the side to see just how upright your back should be.

1 Put your hands on your waist and make a *demi-plié* in 1st position.

2 Spring into the air, pushing up through your feet and stretching your feet and toes.

3 Come down quietly into a *demi-plié* in 1st position, ready to spring again. Now try doing eight at a time.

Galops (sideways)

These are not at all like the Pony *Galops* you learned in Pre-Primary. These travel sideways and a lot of young people know how to do them before they are introduced to a dancing class, but you will learn to place them more carefully now and, if you are clever, to make them light and bouncy. To make them even more difficult you will be joining them to other springing steps. Start in 1st position and then, on the introduction (the part of the music that allows you to get ready), stretch one leg and foot to the side.

1 Hop with your leading leg and foot still stretched sideways and then step on to it.

2 Close your second foot to the first with a spring in the air, toes well pointed (like *sautés*). Come down on your second foot with the leading foot ready to step out again in the same direction. Keep going now until you have reached the other side of the room. Try it with the other leg leading. Can you find a *galop* in another grade?

Exercise for Eye Focus

This is an exercise for the part that your head plays in turning steps. You will find it stops you getting dizzy when you start to turn in the later grades. (Try to find out where that is!) This is the first stage.

Start with your feet parallel (side by side), facing the front of the room with your hands on your waist.

1 Bounce twice without leaving the ground, ending with your knees bent.

2 Turn your head towards the wall to your right and find something in front of you on which to fix your eyes.

3 Spring into the air, turning your whole body a quarter turn to the right to catch up with your head.

Preparation for Character Dancing

Before the end of the class, your teacher will teach you movements which will help you to recognize different musical rhythms. This will be useful in later grades where you will be introduced to Character dancing. There will also be a dance to learn, earning you a chance to show how you can perform. Do you know what that means? It is important to learn how to do this in dancing as it is the way in which to talk to your audience without using words.

Révérence

This is a curtsey for the girls and a bow for the boys, and is the traditional way in which a dancer thanks the teacher for his or her care and encouragement, and the pianist for the music he or she has provided for the class. The curtsey and bow described here will take a slightly different form in later grades, so will not be referred to in detail again.

4 Come down with your feet together and your knees bent, then stretch upwards.

Repeat the exercise to each wall, turning in the same direction each time, until you come back to the front. Now try it all to the left.

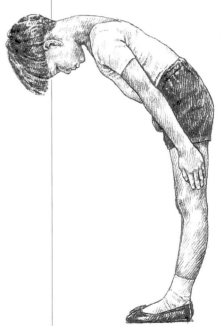

BOW (BOYS)
Start with your feet in 1st position, arms relaxed and hanging by your sides and your head and body held proudly. Step sideways first towards your teacher (or your examiner).

Close your second foot in 1st position and bow your head and shoulders forwards, until your nose almost reaches your knee! Recover carefully to an upright position before stepping to the other side to bow to the pianist.

Révérence

CURTSEY (GIRLS)

Start with your feet in 1st position,
holding your skirt in both hands.

1 Step to the side nearest your teacher (or examiner) first.

2 Close your other foot behind the leg upon which you are standing, with your toes on the floor and your heel raised.

3 Bend your supporting leg carefully, keeping your back and head poised. Stretch the leg upon which you are standing to recover, then repeat the whole curtsey to the other side for the pianist, if one has come to play for you.

Grade One

Now that you have reached this standard, you will begin to work through the class like a professional dancer.

From now on, the exercises are divided into two parts – those taken at the *barre*, and those in the centre. You will have noticed in your dancing class that each grade so far has started with a simple step travelling in a circle. This is designed to get you moving. Each class will continue to begin in this way for the next two grades.

AT THE BARRE

This is where you stand, with either one or two hands lightly resting on a supported bar of wood (or perhaps the back of a chair in your school) which is approximately the same height as your hip. It is here that you will learn to do your basic movements correctly and gain more control over them while being gently supported. Your body should always be held well, with your weight over your feet. On no account should you lean on or pull away from the *barre*.

Demi-plié

As in Primary, this uses 2nd and 1st positions, but in a different time signature. With a *barre* to hold you should be even more successful in keeping your knees sideways over your toes during the downward movement, with your back upright and your head well poised.

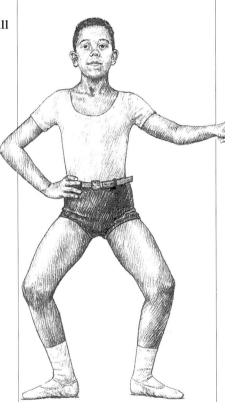

With your feet in 2nd position, bend your knees a little (your teacher will tell you how low to go), pressing them out sideways as you go. Recover. Try this three times before closing to repeat it all in 1st position.

AT THE BARRE

Divided Battements Tendus

Battement means 'beating' and *tendu* means 'stretched'. This exercise is to help lengthen your leg muscles and strengthen the insteps of your feet. In this grade it starts from 1st position and is

taken to the side (2nd position or *à la seconde*), facing the *barre*. To assist you to use your leg and foot correctly the movement is divided, as the title suggests, into four clear stages.

Because a *battement tendu* is such an important movement you will find it in every grade and every professional dancers' class.

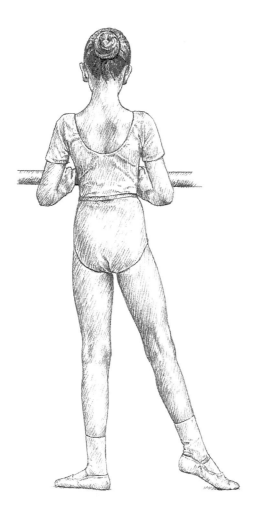 

1 Slide one foot slowly out to the side, until the heel is raised off the floor, but with the toes remaining on the ground. (Keep your weight over your supporting leg; that is, the one upon which you are standing.) Your heel should show some reluctance to come off the floor so that you can use plenty of pressure through your foot.

2 Keeping the inside edge of your heel facing the *barre*, complete the journey to 2nd position by pushing your leg further away and stretching to the ends of your toes.

Stand facing the *barre* with your feet opened out evenly in 1st position. Your hands should be no further apart than your shoulders and the grasp on the *barre* should be light.

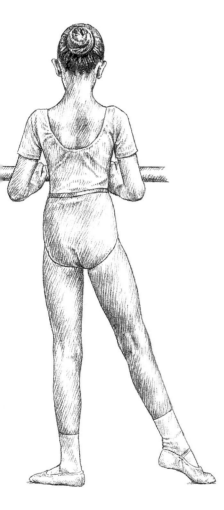

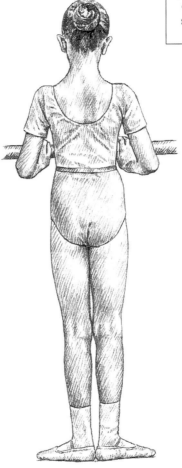

3 To bring your foot back to 1st position, draw your leg in far enough to lower your toes to the ground. Is the inside edge of your heel still facing the *barre*?

4 Continue to draw your leg in towards the other one until your heel has lowered and your foot has closed back to 1st position. This will have taken four counts in all – one count for each stage of the movement. Try it with the other leg and then have a go using only two counts for each *battement tendu*.

IN THE CENTRE

This is where the dancer practises movements without the help of the *barre*, some of which will travel and others which will remain in one place. In each grade, the centre work will start with a relaxation exercise, a different one for each level, just in case the concentration you needed at the *barre* has made you a little tense.

In Grade One, this is followed by an exercise sitting on the floor.

Exercise for Turnout and Flexing

This exercise will strengthen your legs and make your feet more supple. Do you know what that last word means? If not, ask your teacher to explain. Sit as you did for the Primary floor exercise.

1 Rotate your legs in and out as in Primary, then start to curl your toes upwards.

3 Begin to lower the arches of your feet down and away from you, keeping your toes curled up.

R·E·M·E·M·B·E·R

● Keep your back well lifted.

● Make two long, stretched-out legs so your knees do not pop up.

● This is hard work! If you get cramp, stop and wiggle your legs loosely against the ground until it has gone.

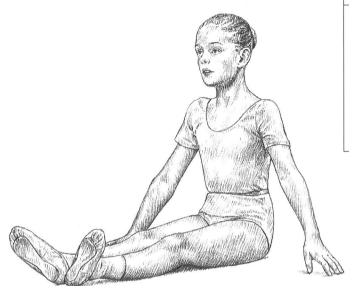

2 Continue to pull your feet in towards your body until they are fully flexed. If you push your leg away from you a little at the same time, your heels may leave the ground. That is all right!

4 Finally, stretch your toes fully to complete the exercise.

IN THE CENTRE

Exercise for Poise

This comes from the Free Movement section of the class and will be combined later with runs.

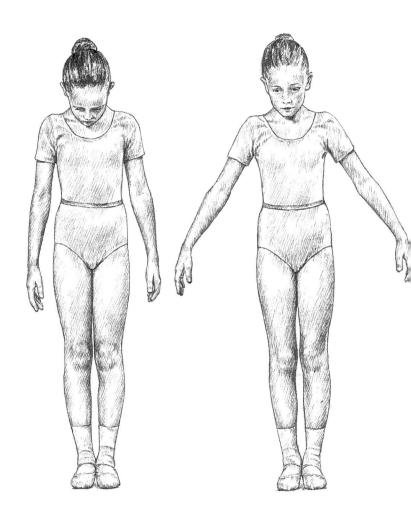

1 Stand with your feet together, arms relaxed at your sides and your head bowed forward.

2 Start to breathe in, raising your head and lifting your arms out sideways as your lungs fill with air. (Do you know where your lungs are? They are situated in the space behind the front of your rib-cage and they act like a pair of bellows.)

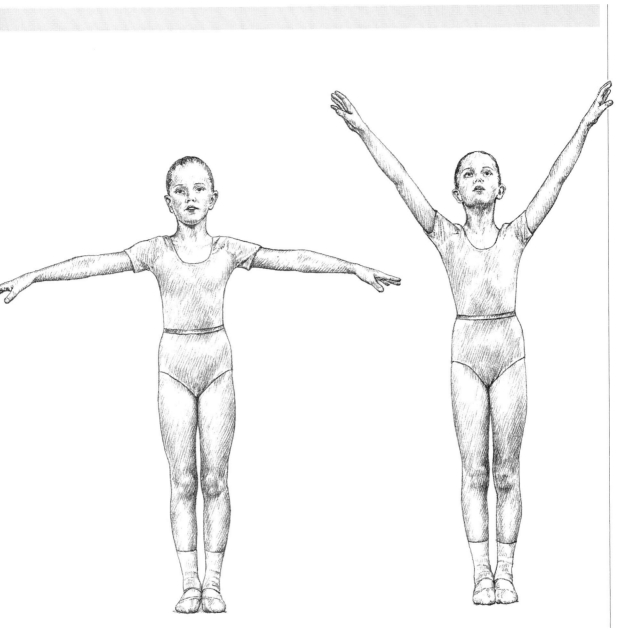

3 At the end of your long, slow, breathe-in, your arms will be fully lifted at your side and your head will be poised on the top of your neck, your eyes gazing upwards and ahead as if looking at the stars in the distance. The height of your head and eyes will depend upon where you can place them without your neck collapsing. Your teacher will help you.

4 Before you explode, gently let the air out of your lungs and return to your starting position. Repeat this another three times, holding the air in the last time and looking as if you are about to lift off gently into space!

IN THE CENTRE

Ports de Bras

The two *ports de bras* in this grade will teach you how to move formally from *bras bas* through 1st, 2nd and 3rd positions as well as *demi-bras*.

Transfer of Weight

Throughout your dancing life, you will be learning how to move the weight of your body from one leg to the other, either slowly or quickly. In this exercise you will be introduced to this movement in a simple way so you can think about your placing and poise too. As the grades progress, this transfer of weight will become more and more complicated, both in its rather static form, as here, and in the development of movement generally.

Your teacher will often talk about it, but in this book the development will only be described briefly in future grades.

Stand in 1st position, arms *bras bas*, facing the front of the room (*en face*).

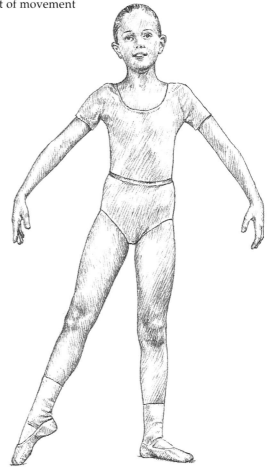

1 Starting with the right leg, do two of the quicker *battements tendus* that you learned earlier at the *barre* to 2nd position. Then slide your leg to the side and hold it there, toes pointed, keeping the weight of your body over the supporting leg. Open your arms sideways to *demi-seconde* to help you balance.

R·E·M·E·M·B·E·R

● Move your body fully from two legs to one leg.

● Keep your back and head well lifted to help the transfer.

● Try not to stiffen up as you do it or your relaxation exercise will have been wasted!

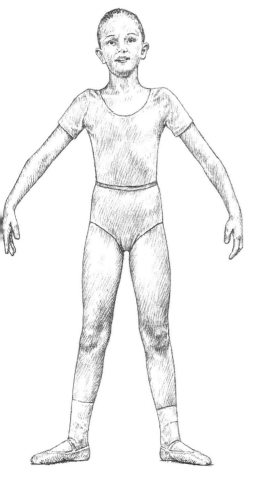

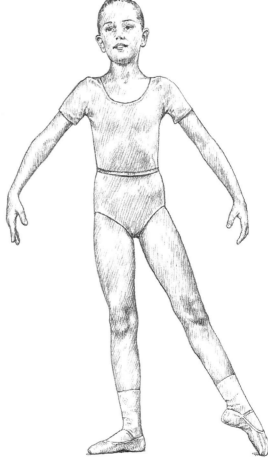

2 Lower your heel in 2nd position, feet evenly turned out and with your body placed in the centre of your feet. Keep your arms still and your head poised.

3 Now push your weight over the leg that started by fully stretching the second leg and foot (the left one) so only your toes remain on the ground. Close your leg to 1st position, lowering your arms back to *bras bas*. Repeat it to the left, then try it all again, introducing a *demi-plié* when your legs are in 2nd position.

IN THE CENTRE

Petits Jetés

Petit means 'little' and *jeté* means 'thrown'. This is a small version of a later step, which consists of springing from one foot to another. Start in 3rd position with your hands on your waist. Get ready to pick up your back foot.

<table>
<tr><td>R·E·M·E·M·B·E·R</td></tr>
</table>

R·E·M·E·M·B·E·R

- Use your legs and feet fully.
- Keep your arms and body still.
- Breathe!
- Bounce!

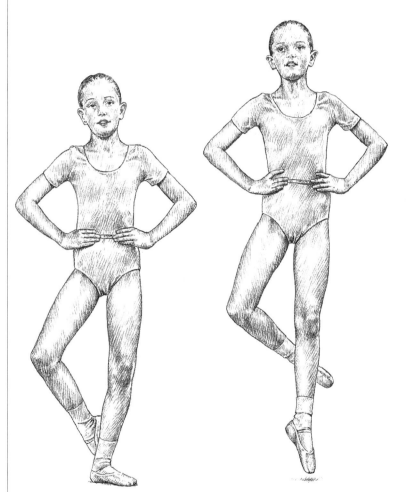

1 Look at the drawing. The right foot is fully pointed with the heel placed closely behind the ankle of the other foot. The knee of the left leg is bent and facing sideways. The right foot is said to be *sur le cou-de-pied* and you will come across this position again in the next grade. See if you can find where.

2 Spring into the air by pushing off on your left leg, stretching your knee and foot fully.

3 Come down softly on to your right leg with the knee bent over your toes, placing the middle of your left foot on the bottom of the plump part of your right lower leg (called the calf). Now try several (at least seven!) *petits jetés* together.

Spring Points

This is another step that springs from one foot to the other. You may have learnt it in the previous grade but, if not, here it is in detail.

You will know already how to point one foot in front with the other leg bent. (Which exercise was that?) Now you are going to add a spring. Start with your feet in 1st position, this time with your arms in *bras bas*. To begin, *demi-plié* in 1st position *en face*.

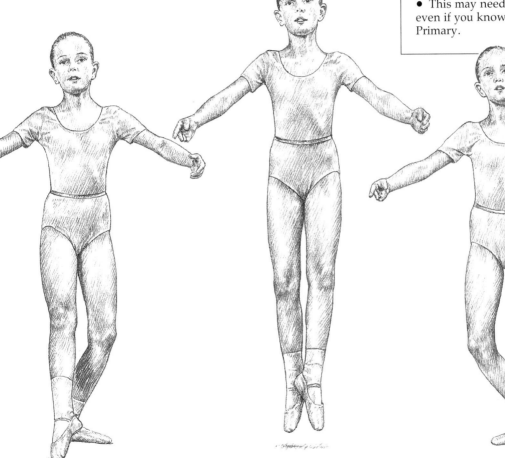

1 Spring into the air and come down with one leg pointed forwards (make it the right leg as in the drawing) and the other leg bent. To steady yourself, lift your arms forward to *demi-bras*.

2 Spring off your left leg and exchange your feet in the air.

3 Come down (quietly) on to a bent right leg, your left leg in front with the toes lightly touching the ground. Try several spring points together now, changing over legs each time.

When you can do these really well, put four together with four *petits jétés*.

IN THE CENTRE

Directions of the Body

Each of the different ways in which the body can face towards an audience has a special name. You have already learned *en face*, the French name for standing square to or facing the front. In this grade, the next step to be described can travel *en ouvert* and your Classical study (a short *enchaînement* of the classical steps you have learned) begins in this direction. Future grades will introduce two more directions, *en croisé* and *en écarté*, so have a look at these illustrations of the directions and use them for future study when you move on to the next level. Any position of the arms can be used for these directions, but use your head and eyes well to add the final touch.

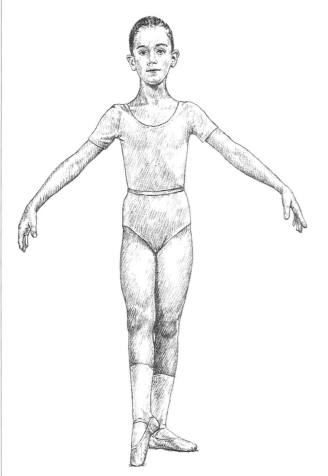

EN FACE (FACING)
Your feet could be in any position on the ground or in the air, as long as your body faces the front.

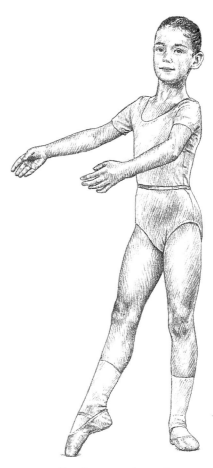

EN OUVERT (OPEN)
One side of your body is turned away from the front, with the leg furthest away from the audience placed in front in 3rd position (or 5th). The front leg could be extended forward (or the back leg to the back) on the ground (*à terre*), or in the air (*en l'air*).

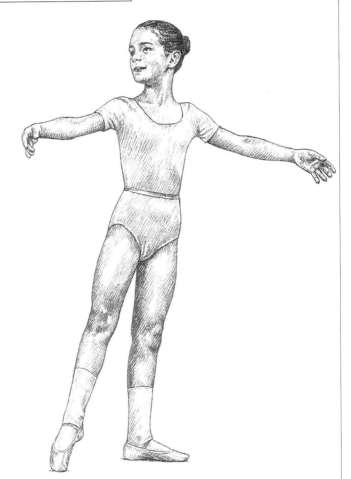

EN CROISÉ (CROSSED)
One side of your body is turned away from the front with the leg nearest the audience crossed in front of the other leg in 3rd position (or 5th). As in *en ouvert*, one leg could be stretched away from the other one.

EN ECARTÉ
(SEPARATED OR THROWN APART)
This can be achieved by stretching one leg to 2nd position with your body turned slightly away from the audience (it could be either leg). Your head will usually be looking over your front shoulder.

IN THE CENTRE

Galops (forwards)

Do you remember *galops* sideways? Both these and *galops* forwards will be used in your Classical study (the little *enchaînement* that you perform towards the end of the class). *Galops* forwards will also be combined with other steps in later grades.

1 Start in one corner of the room, in 3rd position *en ouvert*, arms *bras bas*, ready to travel *en diagonale*. (Where else have you learned to travel along a diagonal line?) Lift your arms to 3rd in opposition – 3rd position with the opposite arm forward to the foot in front. Hop with your leading leg and foot stretched out in front, then step on to it.

2 Close your back foot to your front foot with a spring in the air, toes well pointed. Repeat it along your diagonal, changing your feet after every fourth *galop*. When you change the leading foot, change the arms over too.

Your teacher will show you, separately, how to practise the part where the feet join in the air (*soubresaut*).

RHYTHM AND

If you remember, a part of your Primary class was used to introduce you to different kinds of rhythm and phrasing. From now on this will be added to a section of your class called Character Steps. These are a sophisticated theatrical presentation of a nation's peasant or ethnic dancing. Character dancing is more robust and obviously rhythmical than classical ballet and by learning it you will begin to recognize the differences between the Hungarian, Russian and Polish styles of dancing when you see them performed in the great ballets of the nineteenth century (*Coppelia*, *Swan Lake* and *Sleeping Beauty*). You will also learn to listen to different harmonies, as the music would originally have been played on village instruments. The rhythms that you began to learn in Primary will become more complex, and the steps and movements (including Jumps with Eye Focus) of the style that you are learning will re-appear in the form of a dance at the end of each grade.

The Character steps will need a different sort of shoe, one with a heel and, if you are a girl, you will also wear a longish circular skirt to help you feel the part.

These steps and dances should be fun as they are often done with a partner, and this will help you to get used to dancing with another person. They will also teach you to move in a heavier shoe without clomping around like an old carthorse!

CHARACTER STEPS

Rhythm in 2/4 Time

In this exercise you are going to learn to walk to the beat of a crotchet, in a Hungarian peasant style. Have you changed your shoes? Then place your feet together, facing *en face*, hands on your waist with your fingers forward and your elbows held firmly to the side.

R·E·M·E·M·B·E·R

• Push all your weight over your heel as you step forward so you can balance there for a second.

• Hold your back and head proudly. This will not happen if your elbows have sagged!

• Listen to the rhythm and keep in time.

• Practise the sequence a lot as it is included in your dance.

Révérence

At the end of class, the *révérence* will be in the style of the Character work you have just done and you will therefore remain in your heeled shoes.

1 Step forward firmly on to the heel of your right foot and immediately pick the other foot up off the ground. Lift it well and make sure your foot is pointed. Note at this moment that you have one flexed foot and one pointed foot – that, as well as balancing on your heel, is what makes this step tricky.

2 Lower the toes of your right foot to the ground, allowing your right knee to bend a little. If you are wise you will practise this step at the *barre* first, like the girl in the drawing. Her skirt has been taken off so you can see more clearly how the upper halves of your legs should remain loosely side by side as you pick up your foot. Try with your left foot, then place your feet together and clap three times while you have a rest. Try it all again.

Grade Two

This grade introduces more exercises at the *barre* and a larger vocabulary of movement in the centre. The Character steps remain in Hungary for one more grade, but are increasingly complicated, both in rhythm and style.

AT THE BARRE

Pliés

These will be taken in 1st and 2nd positions, with a *demi-plié* only in the new position, 3rd. Because these are now *grands*, or full, *pliés* you will face the *barre*, holding it with two hands to help you to do the new *pliés* correctly.

A *grand plié* is a full bending of your knees until your thighs (the upper part of the legs) are horizontal with the ground. A *grand plié* always passes through a *demi-plié*, both on the way down and on the way up, which is why you have spent so much time practising the *demi-plié* in previous grades. To begin with, let us look at the *grand plié* in 1st position.

GRAND PLIÉ IN 1ST POSITION
In this position your heels are allowed to rise gradually off the floor, but not until you have reached the depth of the *demi-plié*. The movement downwards should be very smooth, and when you have arrived in the position shown in the picture, your knees should still be over your toes, your back should still be upright and placed over your feet (rather than behind them, which makes you look as if you are going to sit down!) and you should be able to feel all of your toes on the floor.

Having lowered yourself gracefully into the *grand plié*, you must try to rise up out of it with equal grace and control, lowering your heels as soon as possible (without allowing your back to sag or your knees to fall forwards) until your legs are fully stretched. It is important to remember that coming up takes just as long as going down, so there is no jerking of the muscles – they don't like it!

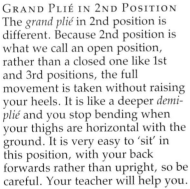

GRAND PLIÉ IN 2ND POSITION
The *grand plié* in 2nd position is different. Because 2nd position is what we call an open position, rather than a closed one like 1st and 3rd positions, the full movement is taken without raising your heels. It is like a deeper *demi-plié* and you stop bending when your thighs are horizontal with the ground. It is very easy to 'sit' in this position, with your back forwards rather than upright, so be careful. Your teacher will help you.

DEMI-PLIÉ IN 3RD POSITION
The *demi-plié* in 3rd position is like the *pliés* you have learned in 1st except that, with one leg in front of the other, it will be a little more difficult to keep your front knee placed over your toes when it is bent. Practise it with both the right and the left foot in front (*devant*).

R·E·M·E·M·B·E·R

- Press your knees sideways over your toes.

- Keep your back upright.

- Keep the movement smooth and even.

- Don't look down to see if you have got it right!

AT THE BARRE

Battements Tendus

You have already learned *battement tendu à la seconde* facing the *barre* in Grade One. Now it will be executed a little faster, sideways to the *barre*, still going through all the stages but without marking them as firmly as before in the music. There should be time to show the arrival of the foot before returning it home. The *battement tendu* will be taken to the front (*devant*) and the back (*derrière*) as well as *à la seconde*, and the journey may start from either 1st or 3rd position when the leg is travelling to the front and the side.

BATTEMENT TENDU DEVANT FROM 1ST POSITION
Your free hand is placed on your waist to remind you about your posture. The arm holding the *barre* should be relaxed and a little in front of your body.

R · E · M · E · M · B · E · R

- Maintain good posture.

- Keep the turnout of your legs and feet even.

- Make the movement smooth.

BATTEMENT TENDU DEVANT
FROM 3RD POSITION
Note the different position of the
working leg.

BATTEMENT TENDU DERRIÈRE
This is more difficult and is
therefore taken facing the *barre*.
The correct positioning of the leg is
easier to find if you begin from 3rd
position.

AT THE BARRE

Battements Glissés

Glisser means 'to slide' or 'to glide'. This is the first time that you have met a *glissé* and it will teach you how to push your leg and foot out quickly and with energy without losing control over it. There are steps in the higher grades, such as *assemblés* and *jetés*, where this movement will prove useful because it will help you to spring high into the air.

At this stage the exercise is taken from 1st position only, with both hands on the *barre* to help you achieve the correct action of the leg without losing your balance. There is a short hold in the middle to allow you time to change legs before trying the movement to the other side. The pointing of your foot should improve if you do this exercise well. Start in 1st position.

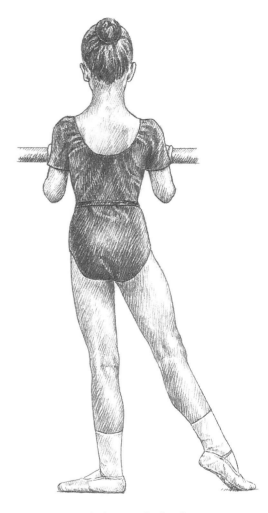

1 With the weight firmly over your supporting leg, begin to push your other foot along the floor, raising the heel so that only the toes remain on the floor.

R · E · M · E · M · B · E · R

• Keep your body still and square to the *barre*.

• Only allow your foot to come off the ground by about 1in (2.5cm). The lower it is, the more clever you have been!

• Try not to look at your foot – feel the right position. Your teacher will help you.

• Watch those hips!

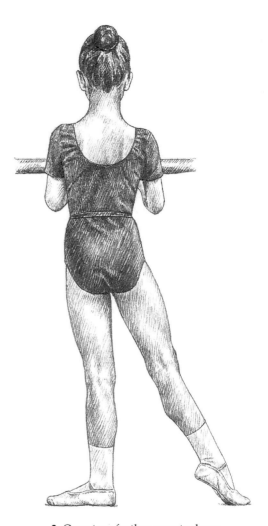

2 Now give your foot an extra nudge. If you use the right amount of energy for this your foot should arrive in 2nd position, just off the ground, beautifully stretched and evenly turned out. There are two counts for this part of the journey.

3 Over two further counts draw your leg home, pausing on the first count to lower your toes back to the ground before pulling your heel firmly back to 1st position. Did your leg arrive home with the feet evenly turned out and relaxed?

In a moment you are going to do it faster, taking only half the number of counts, but first practise it slowly with the other leg. Have you met a movement divided like this before? Where?

AT THE BARRE

Exercise for Battements Fondus

Just as a *demi-plié* assists the steps
that take off from and land on two
feet, so a *fondu* helps you spring
from and alight on one leg without
losing control. As there are many
steps that help you spring from
and alight on one leg, it is a very
serious and important part of your
dance vocabulary.

Fondu means 'melted' and should
indicate to you the way in which
the leg is going to gradually and
slowly give way to a bend.

As *battement fondu* is new to you,
face the *barre* to give yourself
firmer control. Put your feet in 3rd
position. Lift your body well off
your legs before you start.

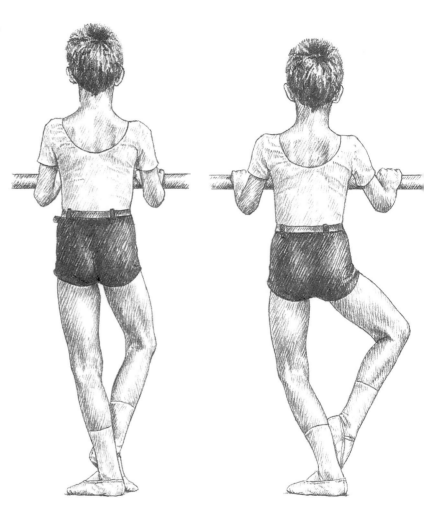

1 Allow your back leg to begin
melting and at the same time start
to peel your front foot off the
ground.

2 At the depth of the *fondu* (like
half a *demi-plié*, that is, without the
heel raised) the front foot will have
arrived in a *cou-de-pied* position
devant. Where have you met this
position before?

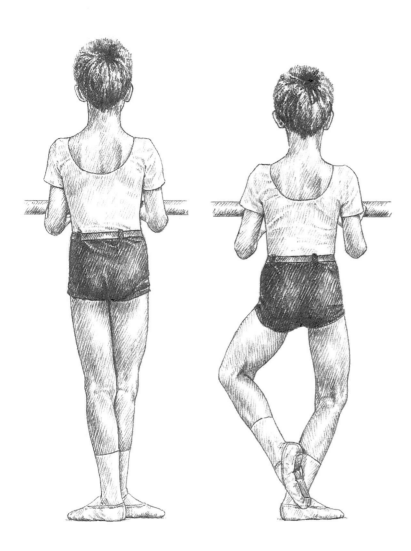

3 Lift out of the *fondu*, straightening your supporting leg as you push your front foot firmly back into 3rd position. Both knees should now be stretched.

During both the downward and the upward movements, your legs should arrive at their destination at the same moment.

4 Now try lifting your back foot as you *fondu*. When you have arrived, check that both knees are over your toes, particularly the one that is lifted, as it may be more unstable than the other one. Recover as before.

Try the *fondu devant* again and, this time, as you straighten the supporting leg extend the other leg from the *cou-de-pied* to 2nd position, hold it for a moment and then close to 3rd position *derrière*. Are you ready to repeat it all to the other side?

R·E·M·E·M·B·E·R

● Support your back as you melt.

● Press your knees away from each other in the *fondu*.

● Squeeze your legs together gently on the recovery.

AT THE BARRE

Grands Battements

Grand means 'big' or 'large' and describes the large throwing action which will help to loosen your leg at the hip joint (do you remember where that is?) A *grand battement* starts like a *battement glissé* but, because of the extra energy you are going to use, your leg will be forced higher into the air, even above your waistline! But that will not happen here, where you are going to learn first to throw your leg and then control its descent.

Stand sideways to the *barre* with your feet in 3rd position and your free hand on your waist.

GRAND BATTEMENT DEVANT
1 Begin the throwing action forward with a movement like a *glissé* to make sure your leg and foot are fully stretched.

R·E·M·E·M·B·E·R

- Throw your working leg without disturbing your supporting one.

- Keep your back still.

- Keep your knees tight.

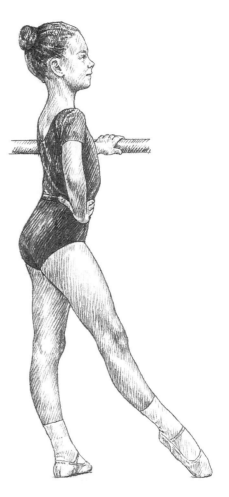

2 Continue to throw your foot upwards until your leg refuses to go higher. The height of this throw will depend on how loose you are and, therefore, it may not be the same as your friends'. Do not be tempted to cheat by bending your supporting leg to make your other leg go higher! It will simply make your back curl up like a hedgehog's.

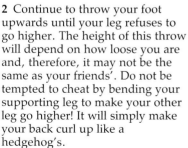

3 After the throw, lower your leg with control to a pointed foot on the ground and then slide the foot back to 3rd position, ready to start again. Try this three times and then *demi-plié* to give your legs a rest. Repeat it all again.

Grand battement is also taken *à la seconde* in this grade. As it is a harder position than the one illustrated here, face the *barre* and begin from 1st position to help the turnout of your working leg. Do three at a time, then rest before repeating with the other leg.

AT THE BARRE

Rises

Rises help you to strengthen the trunk of your body, legs and feet in preparation for *pirouettes* and, later, *pointe* work. In Grade Two they are done slowly to give you plenty of time to pull the weight of your body over the ball (or pad) of each foot while keeping all your toes in contact with the ground.

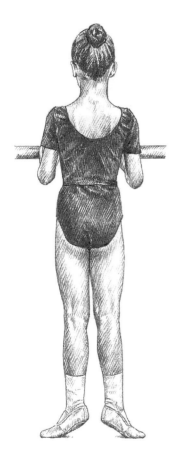
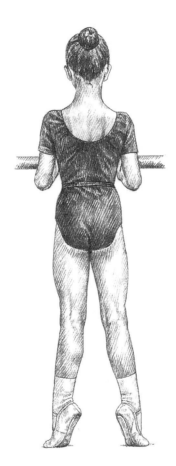

1 Face the *barre* in 1st position. Firstly, lift right through your back (without the help of your shoulders) and imagine the top of your head is being sucked towards the ceiling by a giant magnet. This will assist you to start rising to a position called *quarter-pointe* without lurching forwards. Spread your toes out evenly inside your shoes.

2 Continue to pull upwards until your heels have lifted as far as they can go without peeling your toes off too (*half-pointe*). Watch that your knees do not begin to give in at this point. Stretch them into a straight line and make sure both your big and little toes are in contact with the floor. If either one is tempted to lift off, the line of your leg will be weakened at the ankle and make you unsafe and wobbly.

3 Now mentally place a large spring under each heel and begin to press down on to it until you have lowered to a *quarter-pointe*. Hold on to your turnout or it might disappear! Then gently lower your heels to the ground.

Try it three times, then rest with a *demi-plié* before you start again. As you can see, imagination is going to play a big part in what appears to be a simple movement, although it is hard to do well.

IN THE CENTRE

As usual, this begins with a relaxation exercise. Pay attention to the way your arms are used in it because this movement will re-appear later on.

Ports de Bras

Again there are two of these, one to teach you to move through 5th position, the other to introduce you informally to an *arabesque* line (2nd position). (*Arabesques* will be described in Grade Three.)

Battements Tendus with Transfer of Weight

This is similar to the exercise that you did in Grade One but it begins in a new direction, *en croisé*. Look back to pages 40-41 if you do not remember how to place it.

Changements

This is another springing step. It means 'changing'. Start with your feet in 3rd position *en face*, arms *bras bas*. (You will have practised springing with your arms in this position in the previous grade.)

R·E·M·E·M·B·E·R
● Keep your posture upright.
● Keep your arms still – don't heave yourself into the air with them.
● Lower your heels firmly in *demi-plié*.

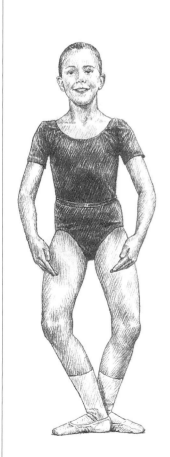

1 *Demi-plié*, right foot in front, arms *bras bas*.

2 Push off into the air, fully stretching your legs and feet.

3 Come down quietly with the left foot in front in 3rd position. You are going to add this step to the next one in a moment.

IN THE CENTRE

Echappés Sautés to 2nd (à la seconde)

The boys have a slightly different sequence of movements to the girls but basically it is the same step.

Echapper means 'to escape'. The step begins with a spring which looks like the middle part of a *galop* forwards, where the feet are joined in the air, one behind the other. At this point they 'escape' from each other.

1 Start in *demi-plié* in 3rd position, arms *bras bas*.

2 Spring into the air, pulling one foot over the other, beginning to open your arms sideways.

3 Open your feet and come down in *demi-plié* in 2nd position – not *too* wide – with your arms in *demi-seconde* to steady yourself.

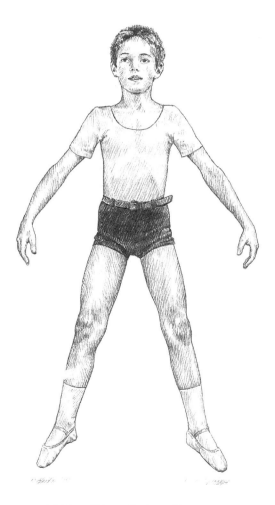

4 Take off from 2nd position, stretching your legs and feet well. Keep your arms in *demi-seconde*.

5 Alight (come down) in *demi-plié* in 3rd position with your left foot in front and your arms *bras bas*.

IN THE CENTRE

Unfolding Skips (Free Movement)

Now that you have reached Grade Two, perhaps we should talk about 'Free' Movement in more detail. Although it does not use turnout, Free Movement does require good use of the legs and feet and will need a pleasing line throughout the body, arms and head. It will also require a good sense of movement and this might all be achieved more easily if you occasionally try to do it without shoes and socks (or tights).

These skips travel round in a circle, so you can keep going! Start with your feet together, but with the weight over the left leg, and the right foot relaxed and ready to go. Let your arms hang naturally at your sides.

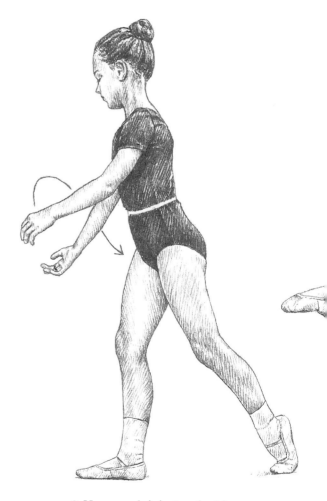

1 Step out well on your right foot, swinging both arms across your body to the right.

2 Hop your left foot up beside your right leg, beginning to swing your arms up and over in a circular path (not *too* high).

Arms for Unfolding Skips

Here in more detail is the path of
the arms. They form a figure-8 as
in the relaxation exercise.

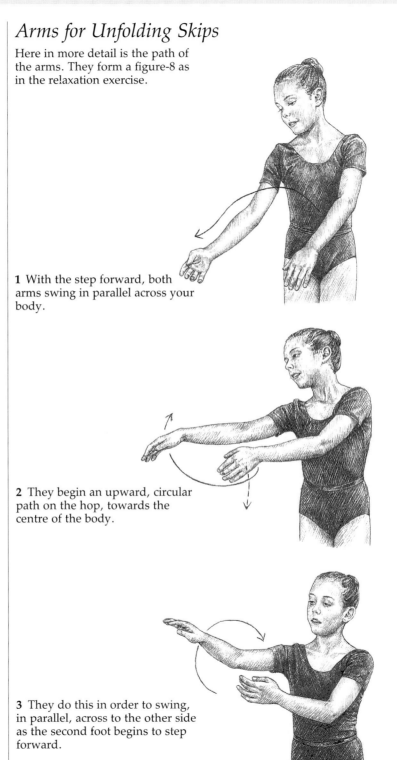

1 With the step forward, both
arms swing in parallel across your
body.

2 They begin an upward, circular
path on the hop, towards the
centre of the body.

3 Unfold your left leg in a forward
direction ready to step out and
forwards. Begin to swing your
arms across your body to the left.

3 They do this in order to swing,
in parallel, across to the other side
as the second foot begins to step
forward.

69

IN THE CENTRE

Coupés

Coupé means 'cut' and refers to cutting away the weight from one foot to another with a slight spring. In this grade it is combined with *galops* forward.

1 Stand on your right leg with your knees bent and your left foot *derrière* in *cou-de-pied*. Arms *demi-seconde*.

2 Spring off your right leg into the air with one foot behind the other, both knees straight, like the beginning of *echappés sautés*.

3 Come down quietly on your left leg with your right foot in *cou-de-pied devant*. Now reverse it.

Galops with Attitude

This is a step designed to help you to get off the ground (elevate). It is taken in a circle to give you the opportunity to try it several times without stopping.

Start in 3rd position and, on the introduction of the music, *dégagé* the foot *devant*. (*Dégagé* means 'disengaged' and all you do is stretch your foot out without bringing it home again, as you would if it were a *battement tendu*.) Hop and *galop* forwards with the arms in 3rd opposition.

An *attitude* is a balletic position said to have been invented by Blasis, who was inspired by the statue of Mercury by Giovanni da Bologna.

Studies

You have the choice of performing a Classical study, a collection of the steps you have learned in this and previous grades or a short dance reflecting all the Free Movements you have studied.

1 Step forward on your right foot and begin to change your arms over to 3rd with the other arm in opposition.

2 Swish your left foot through and hop, lifting your left leg forward to a position called *attitude devant*. This is like a *grand battement devant* with your leg fore-shortened at the knee, pulling the foot in towards the centre of the body. The thigh is turned out as it would be in a *grand battement devant* and you should almost be able to sit a cup and saucer on your left ankle!

RHYTHM AND CHARACTER STEPS

Continuing with the Hungarian peasant style, here is a step called *pas de basque and cifra.*

Pas de basque and cifra

This is danced holding hands with a partner. Change into your character shoes (and skirt, if you are a girl) and start with your feet parallel *en face*, boy with his hand on his waist, girl holding out her skirt.

The feeling should be one of pummelling the ground rather than springing energetically into the air. The *pas de basque* turns a little away from your partner and then towards him or her. Acknowledge your partner on the inward turn!

All these steps can travel forward on count 'one', in which case keep the whole sequence *en face*.

PAS DE BASQUE
1 Spring gently on to the foot furthest away from your partner, releasing the other one from the ground. Do not travel sideways – keep on the spot (*sur place*). This is count 'one'.

2 Transfer your weight briefly and silently on to the ball of the second foot on 'and'. Place it close to the middle of the other foot.

3 Quietly return your weight to the first foot, relaxing your knee on 'a'.

Repeat all these steps, leading with the inside foot and then repeat again with the other foot (four times in all).

RHYTHM AND CHARACTER STEPS

CIFRA

Now for the cifra, viewed a little from the side, to show clearly the position of the foot.

This is the same as the *pas de basque*, except that on 'and' you are going to transfer the weight silently on to the heel of the second foot rather than the ball. Girls will now have their hands on their waists.

The four cifra *sur place* turn a little away and towards your partner, like the *pas de basque,* but remain *en face* if you travel forwards on the first step.

Jumps with Eye Focus

The Jumps with Eye Focus, which now involve a half-turn, are taken as an exercise on their own and are involved in the Character dance which ends the class.

Révérence

Again, a Character *révérence* will thank your teacher and pianist.

Grade Three

This is a difficult grade, full of technical hurdles, but if you can overcome them you are well on your way to the next grade. In this grade go straight to the *barre*.

AT THE BARRE

Pliés

These are taken sideways to the *barre* in 1st and 2nd positions, as in Grade Two, but with an arm movement and also the addition of a *grands plié* in 3rd position. As before, there is a mixture of *demi* and *grands pliés* in your exercise with a simple *port de bras* in between the different positions of the feet.

GRAND PLIÉ IN 3RD POSITION
The *grand plié* in 3rd position is done in the same way as 1st position but with one extra point to think about – on the downward movement, do not let your heels slip backwards. If you have done it correctly you will feel your back heel pressing slightly against the front one. Don't look – just try to feel it.

You will see from the drawing that, on the descent, the arm opens gently from *bras bas* to *demi-seconde* with the eyes following the hand. On the stretch up the arm is drawn back to *bras bas*.

R · E · M · E · M · B · E · R

- Make the movement continuous from beginning to end.

- Don't let your heels pop up! Only raise them as far as they need to go.

- Try to keep your back upright while using your arm. You may be tempted to lean towards it.

AT THE BARRE

Battements Tendus and Battements Glissés

These are done in two counts now, sideways to the *barre*, taken from 3rd position only and executed to the front, to the side and then to the back. This sequence of movements is called *en croix*, which means 'in the shape of a cross'.

Ronds de Jambe à Terre

This is a circular movement of one leg, on the ground. When the circle is made outwards it is called *en dehors* and when inwards it is called *en dedans*. If you keep your knee turned sideways throughout the circular action, it will help to loosen your leg at the hip joint and increase your turnout. In this grade it is a preparation only, so there are four counts for each circle.

2 Carry your leg, fully stretched, round to 2nd position, keeping your toes on the ground (one count). Is your knee still equally turned out?

EN DEHORS
1 From 1st position, slide your outside leg forwards until your foot is fully pointed (one count). Your free arm is in 2nd position and will stay there throughout.

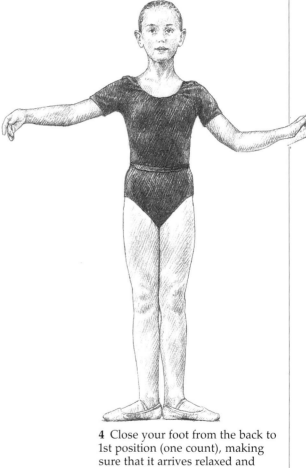

3 Continue to circle your stretched leg and foot round to the back, toes still on the ground, until your heel is opposite 1st position (one count).

4 Close your foot from the back to 1st position (one count), making sure that it arrives relaxed and without allowing the ankle to drop forwards.

Now try it all the other way round, *en dedans*, taking your leg to the back first. You may find this circle a little more difficult because your thigh has to work harder to keep your knee facing outwards.

AT THE BARRE

Battements Fondus

This is the same exercise as in Grade Two except that it is taken sideways to the *barre* and is repeated in reverse (that is, starting again with the back foot).

Retirés

Retiré means 'withdrawn'. This is another new movement and it is going to form the beginning of another new exercise called *développé* which appears later on.

Retiré also appears in a springing step in this grade. Can you discover which one? Stand in 1st position facing the *barre*.

1 Release one foot from the floor, fully pointed.

2 Draw your thigh up gradually in 2nd position while sliding your pointed toes to the hollow just at the back of your supporting knee. All this so far takes two counts.

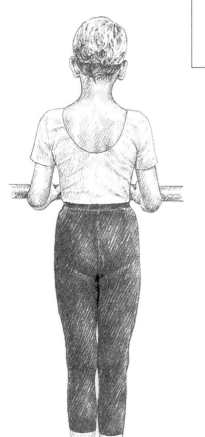

R·E·M·E·M·B·E·R

● Keep your hips square to the *barre* to make sure the turnout is even on both legs.

● Be just as careful, on the quicker *retirés*, to keep the toes of your working foot in contact with the other leg and stretch the working knee fully in between the two.

Sickle Foot

Keep your heel forwards in line with your lower leg, both on the way up and on the way down, otherwise it will form a 'sickle', or twist, at the ankle.

3 Carefully slide your foot down your supporting leg until the working knee is fully stretched and your foot is back in 1st position. (This takes another two counts.)

Now see if you can do it twice in half the time (two counts each *retiré*). Then try with the other leg.

AT THE BARRE

Grands Battements Derrière

Grands battements devant and *à la seconde* are combined in this grade, but as those *derrière* are new they are taken on their own, facing the *barre*. There is one extra point to learn about a *grand battement* when demonstrated *derrière*. This is the first time that you have raised your leg so high off the ground to the back. In order to do so, your body must tilt forwards slightly from the top of the supporting leg, before recovering to its upright position on the close. Your teacher will help you to find the right amount of tilt and will, at the same time, make sure you have not pulled your body backwards off the leg upon which you are standing.

1 Start in 3rd position. As before, begin the throwing action backwards with a *glissé* movement to fully extend your leg. Make sure that your foot remains behind the hip of your working leg for correct placing. (The hip is the bony part that juts out between your hip joint and your waist.) Continue to throw your leg in an upward motion, tilting forwards a little as needed. The higher the throw the further the tilt.

R·E·M·E·M·B·E·R

- Keep your leg behind you.
- Keep both knees tight.
- Try not to pull away from the *barre*.

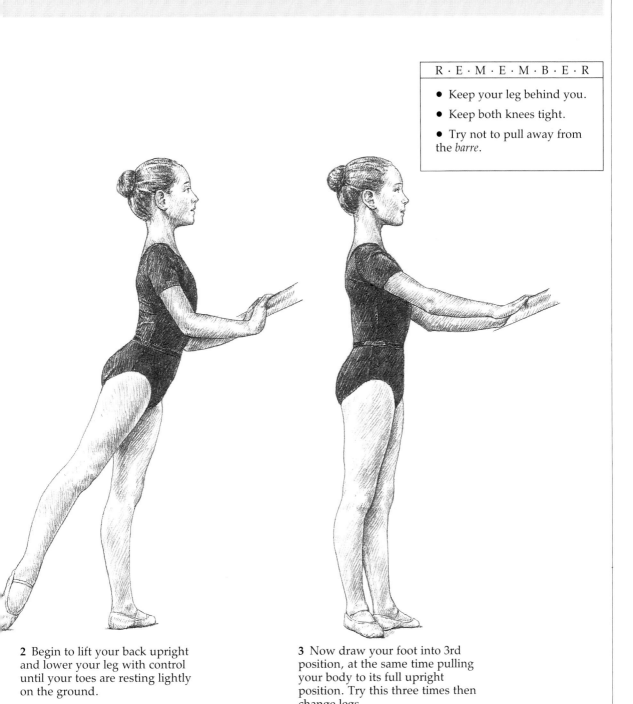

2 Begin to lift your back upright and lower your leg with control until your toes are resting lightly on the ground.

3 Now draw your foot into 3rd position, at the same time pulling your body to its full upright position. Try this three times then change legs.

AT THE BARRE

Developpés Devant

Developpé means 'developed' and the movement consists of a slow unfolding (or developing) of one leg. It is practised at the *barre* to gain strength, control and balance so that, when in the centre, you will be able to unfold your leg into any position and hold it there.

1 Start in 3rd position, arms *bras bas*. Raise your front foot until it is fully pointed and slide it up the front of your supporting leg to a position just below your knee. At the same time, lift your arm to 1st position. Keep your thigh in 2nd position, just as you do in the *retiré* exercise.

2 Holding your thigh at the same height, begin to unfold your leg by pushing the lower half forward first, so you keep the turnout already established in the hip joint. Begin to open your arm to 2nd position.

R·E·M·E·M·B·E·R

- Hold your turnout equally in both thighs.

- Listen to the music – it will help you with the unfolding.

- Practise until you can do this exercise with ease. A pained expression is not attractive in a dancer!

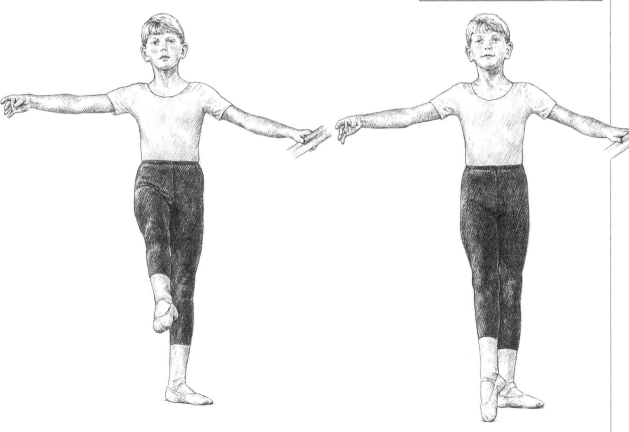

3 Stretch your leg fully in the air, taking care to ease your knee into position so you do not jar the joint. Hold it there for a moment with your arm in 2nd position.

4 Keeping your back supported, lower your leg slowly until your pointed foot reaches the ground, holding your arm in 2nd position to retain the lift in your upper body. Close with pressure to 3rd position, lowering your arm gently to *bras bas*.

AT THE BARRE

Rises

These are now twice as fast as Grade Two and, in addition, start from 3rd position. Keep your back heel in close contact with the front one, both on the upward movement and the descent.

Exercise for Relevés Devant and Pirouette Position

Relevé means *'lifted'* or *'raised up'*. The *relevé* in this exercise serves as a preparation for *pirouettes* (turns on one leg), as it will help you to strengthen your legs, feet and torso (the trunk of the body) so you can spin *and* stay in control. It will also begin to prepare the girls for *pointe* work (when special shoes are worn to protect your toes). Because it is a new movement, it will face the *barre*.

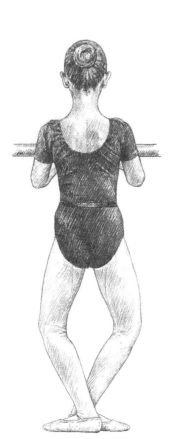

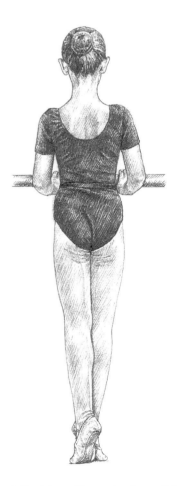

RELEVÉS DEVANT
1 Start in 3rd position. *Demi-plié* in 3rd position.

2 Pushing off your heels, swiftly straighten your knees and pull, or snatch, your feet firmly together on to *demi-pointe* (or half-point), drawing both in close together so one foot is behind the other. Imagine you are wearing a tight-fitting garment around your waist and ribs to lift your body without the aid of your shoulders.

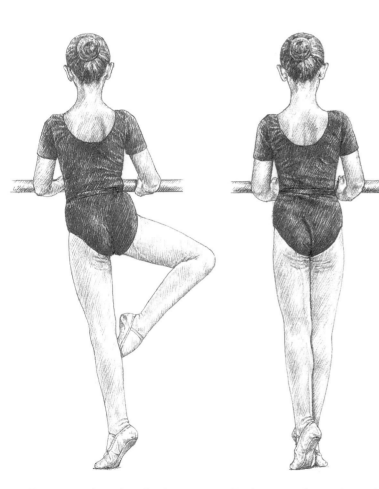

3 Draw your front foot firmly to a position similar to the one you made in *developpé* before you unfolded your leg (*pirouette* position). Press the working thigh to the side.

4 Replace your foot to its position on *demi-pointe*, straightening your knee carefully but firmly. Now lower both heels with a slight spring to allow your feet to open out to 3rd position in *demi-plié*. Try this twice more, then *dégagé* ('disengage') your front foot to 2nd position, close *derrière* and begin again with the other foot in front.

PIROUETTE POSITION
Take a closer look at the *pirouette* position. To find *pirouette* position, cradle the kneecap of your supporting leg with the instep, or arch, of your other foot. Look to see if you have found the right place and then try not to look again. Take your hands off the *barre* from time to time to see if you can balance in this position.

IN THE CENTRE

The relaxation exercise in this grade is good for slimming the waist! It also teaches you to swing your arms with weight and to achieve a good stretch of the arms through the shoulder line.

Ports de Bras

This introduces you informally to a different *arabesque* line (3rd).

Battements Tendus en Croix

These are taken as you did them at the *barre*, with your arms placed in a way that will assist you to balance. There is a little surprise in between, not exactly a *pirouette* but something like it. Do you remember what *en croix* means?

Classical Walks with Arabesque

Classical walks are a development of the walks that you learned in Pre-Primary and Primary. During Grades One and Two you will have continued to learn how to walk gracefully and elegantly – proudly if you are a boy – both quickly and slowly on two different diagonals. Now these walks are going to serve as an introductory movement to an *arabesque*.

An *arabesque* consists of balancing on one leg with the other extended behind, the arms in a position to create the longest oblique, or slanted line, possible between your

1 Having taken two slow and elegant walks forward (one *en ouvert* and one *en croisé* as you are travelling along a diagonal again, at the same time lifting your arms slowly through *bras bas* to 1st position), prepare to step forward on your left foot with your right knee flexed (slightly bent) ready to push your weight forward.

1ST ARABESQUE
2 To make a 1st *arabesque*, push off your back leg until it is stretched out behind with a fully arched foot, stepping on to a well turned out, straight supporting leg. Place your left arm forwards in an upwards oblique line, your right arm sloping down and just behind 2nd position. Both palms will be facing down. Lift your head and look over the fingertips of your forward arm. Recover by opening your arms to 2nd position, then bring them to *bras bas* as you close your back foot to 1st position.

finger tips and your toes. This has to be done without the aid of your shoulders or hips, which remain square to the line of direction. The oblique line curves slightly at your body and, as usual, your head and eyes provide the finishing touches.

Arabesque is one of the most well-known positions in ballet. It is usually viewed sideways, or almost sideways, to see the dancer's outline at its best. There are many different *arabesques* that can be performed slowly, or quickly as part of a springing step (you will find an example in your

Classical study later on). You will be using two *arabesques* in this exercise, 1st and 2nd, but as you were informally introduced to 3rd *arabesque* in your *ports de bras* a description of that will be included too.

2ND ARABESQUE

3 Prepare for 2nd *arabesque* in the same way, this time lifting your opposite (right) arm forwards to your supporting leg, a little lower this time in order not to cover your face. Place the other arm as for 1st *arabesque*. Make sure your hips and shoulders are square. Look forwards towards the little finger of your right hand this time. Recover as before.

3RD ARABESQUE

4 3rd *arabesque* is like putting 1st and 2nd together (1 + 2 = 3). Prepare as before, taking your left arm forward to 1st *arabesque* and the right forward to 2nd *arabesque*, eyes looking over the top arm. Now try it all stepping forwards into *arabesque* on your right leg. Change diagonals so you are stepping *en ouvert* again. (Just to remind you, 3rd *arabesque* is not combined with your Classical walks in this grade, but you could practise it that way!)

R · E · M · E · M · B · E · R

- Bring your shoulders forward over your supporting leg on the transfer of weight.

- Hold your posture firmly.

- Make the longest line possible without making your *arabesque* look like a cardboard cut-out.

- Feel elegant!

IN THE CENTRE

Triple Runs

These come from the Free Movement section and are taken in an anti-clockwise circle (what does that mean?) When you start to learn these runs try them in bare feet so you can get a good grip on the floor and really feel the use of your legs and feet as well as the movement forwards. Triple runs are given their name because they consist of three movements. It might help, to begin with, to think of them as long walks and then, as you speed them up, they will have more of the quality of running. Start with your feet parallel (side by side), arms relaxed and hanging at your sides.

R·E·M·E·M·B·E·R

• Each run is of equal length and will therefore produce a smooth and fast-moving motion forwards. You should create a draught as you go by!

• Keep your arms moving in a clearly defined shape (figure-8 over two triple runs) and in a relaxed manner!

• This is supposed to be enjoyable!

1 Take a long step forwards on your right leg, with your toes reaching the ground before your heel. Oops! Here comes that difficult arm movement again from the unfolding skips in Grade Two. Lift both arms over to the right in a small circular and downward movement, head following.

2 Making an equally long stride (step out) forwards on to the ball of your left foot, with your heel only just raised, begin to lift your arms upwards, head following.

3 Take another long step forwards on the ball of your right foot, heel just raised, lifting both arms over to the centre of your body, head still following.

Repeat it all, beginning with your left foot and making half a figure-8 to the left with both arms, palms open and following the movement of your arms. This will be combined in your Free Movement study, if you choose to do that rather than the Classical one, with unfolding skips from Grade Two.

IN THE CENTRE

Exercise for Pirouettes

Having continued to develop the
Jumps with Eye Focus until this
grade, your head is now prepared
for this exercise. Do not forget the
pirouette position that you learned
at the *barre*. Start in 3rd position,
arms *bras bas*.

1 *Relevé* on to two feet, one behind
the other, as at the *barre*. Then
demi-plié with a slight spring as
before. Raise your arms to 1st
position and hold them there.

2 *Relevé devant* from the *demi-plié*
straight to *pirouette* position,
placing your arms in 3rd. Return to
demi-plié, retaining the arms.
Quickly release your back foot.

3 Step up on to the back foot, releasing the front one, arms closing to 1st position, and begin a rapid exchange of weight from the ball of one foot to the other (this is known as *courus*, tiny rapid runs), making a whole circle to the right, then *demi-plié*, arms *bras bas*. Repeat it all, then pause and repeat to the left.

4 The boy has a slightly different sequence of events, and his hands are placed on his waist to assist the lift in the body.

IN THE CENTRE

Balancés de Côté

Balancer means 'to rock or sway' and *de côté* means 'from side to side', so this is a step which rocks sideways with the head, body and arms swinging in unison. Listen to the music. It is a waltz and will help you to keep the rocking motion smooth. Stand on your left leg and cross the ball of your right foot behind your supporting leg so one calf is resting against the other. Arms are *demi-seconde*.

BALANCÉS DE CÔTÉ (GIRLS)
1 Slide your right leg out to 2nd position with your arms in *demi-seconde*. Push firmly off your left leg, sending the other a little further along the floor and lifting yourself slightly into the air, until both feet are fully stretched. Begin to lift your arms a little, head erect. Breathe in!

2 Shift your weight over and bend your right leg, lowering the heel to the ground, sweeping your left arm across to 3rd position and following it with your head and eyes. Your body will be tilted slightly sideways to the right – this is count 'one'.

3 Bring your left foot in behind your right ankle and momentarily take your weight on to the ball of your left foot, holding your arms still and beginning to stretch the instep of your right foot – this is count 'two'.

4 Before your right foot has time to fully stretch, lower your weight on to it again – count 'three'. Do it all again the other way, leaning your head and body to the left and changing your arms over. Try several *balancés de côté* together.

IN THE CENTRE

BALANCÉS DE CÔTÉ (BOYS)
Apart from starting in 3rd position, right foot *derrière*, the boys' version has the same footwork as the girls', but should look firmer and more extended. It also has a different arm movement. Start with your hands on your hips.

R·E·M·E·M·B·E·R
• Step out well on the first movement.
• Make the lilting movement gentle.
• Finish transferring your arms from one side to the other a little later than your feet to give a sense of continuous movement.

Pas de Chat

This means 'step of the cat' and is so-called because of its light, cat-like quality. It can be seen in many of the classical ballets, in particular *Sleeping Beauty* where there are two dancers dressed as cats, and in

1 As you step out from your left foot to your right, turn your shoulders to the right and sweep your right arm forwards and out to 2nd position with the palm upwards. Follow with your head and eyes and keep them still on counts 'two' and 'three'.

2 With your *balancé* to the left, turn your shoulders to the left, sweeping your right arm forward and across your body with the palm downwards. Follow with your head and eyes as before. Try several more.

1 Raise your right leg rapidly to *retiré* while pushing off your left until it is fully stretched, in order to give height to your spring.

Swan Lake where the four cygnets do a series of sixteen *pas de chats* across the stage. Next time you go to the ballet, look out for them. Start in 3rd position *en face*, arms in 3rd opposition.

Practise several *pas de chats* – for example, twice with a stretch and bend of the knees in between. Then try one followed immediately by a *changement* and a stretch bend so you can practise beginning with the other leg travelling to the left.

R · E · M · E · M · B · E · R

● Don't just lift your knees to your ears – spring!

● Keep your steps quiet, light and stealthy. Study a cat!

● Make sure the second foot that lifts to *retiré* is fully pointed and that your thigh remains sideways.

2 Quickly bend your left leg up to *retiré*, as if chasing your right foot with your left.

3 Land quietly on your right leg, *en fondu*, beginning to lower the other one quickly. Finish in *demi-plié*, left foot *devant*.

IN THE CENTRE

Jetés Ordinaires

The basic spring from one foot to
the other (*petit jeté*) plus the speedy
sliding action of one leg has
already been tackled. Now it is
time to put them together!

1 Start in 3rd position *en face*, arms
bras bas and *demi-plié*.

2 Begin to make a swishing
movement, like a *battement glissé*,
to 2nd position with your back
foot. As it reaches its full extent,
push off your supporting leg,
using the 'swish' to help you up.

R·E·M·E·M·B·E·R

• Keep your 'swish' under control. The stronger and lower it is, the more help it will be. A *grand battement* movement is only useful if you are going to use the step to travel sideways.

• Avoid heaving with your arms and back. Keep the top half of your body still and leave the work to your legs and feet.

• Breathe!

3 Spring into the air, fully pointing your foot underneath and keeping the other leg still.

4 Draw your swishing leg in on the way down so that on landing it replaces your other foot. Bend your other leg up, thigh to the side with your foot fully pointed behind the middle of your supporting calf.

To repeat the *jeté* to the other side, lower your foot to the ground in order to make a *battement glissé* movement to the other side, passing through 3rd position on the way. Try now with a hop in between and, when you feel confident, add a few *coupés*.

IN THE CENTRE

Exercise for Grand Allegro

Allegro is the grown-up term for
the part of your class that begins to
move, firstly with *petit allegro* or
the small steps and followed by
grand allegro, the steps that require
more elevation. This exercise is
designed to help you with these
bigger steps.

1 Start *en ouvert* with your right leg
dégagé devant, arms *demi-seconde*,
ready to travel *en diagonale*. Take a
good step forward on your right
leg, beginning to swing your arms
down and forward through *bras
bas*. Look straight ahead.

2 Continuing to swing your arms
up to 1st position, throw your left
leg forward to an extension *devant*
and *temps levé* (hop!), travelling in
the air along your diagonal. Your
arm and leg should be co-
ordinated – they should happen
together to help pull your body up
high into the air.

3 Alight on your right leg, leaving
your arms in 1st position to help
brace your back.

R·E·M·E·M·B·E·R

● This is terrific fun to do, but don't let your enthusiasm undermine your control.

● For instance, keep your arms low and correctly placed.

● Do not be tempted to kick the first leg too high. Remember the hedgehog effect!

4 Step forward on your left leg, beginning to swing your arms down towards *bras bas*.

5 *Temps levé* on your left leg, opening your arms to *demi-seconde*, and place your right foot to a *retiré derrière*, foot to the back of your knee. Again co-ordinate your arms with your legs to gain the maximum height allowed within your music. Look out triumphantly to the audience!

Continue now until you run out of diagonal, then try with the other leg leading, not forgetting to change your diagonal line.

RHYTHM AND CHARACTER STEPS

The style now changes to Russian and one of the aims of this section in Grade Three is to develop a feeling for *staccato* (sharp) and *legato* (continuous, unbroken) movements.

Hop Steps

These come under the heading of a *staccato* movement. They travel round the room. Place your feet parallel and put the knuckles of your hands on your hips, fingers curled into the palm of each hand and held there by your thumb. (Have you changed your shoes?)

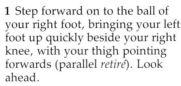

R·E·M·E·M·B·E·R
• Keep the rhythm even.
• Pick your foot up sharply to your knee and keep your elbows strong and slightly forwards.
• Travel well – create a draught!
• There should be no noise except on the stamps.

1 Step forward on to the ball of your right foot, bringing your left foot up quickly beside your right knee, with your thigh pointing forwards (parallel *retiré*). Look ahead.

2 Hold this position and skim forwards over the surface of the floor, keeping your right knee stretched and the ankle tight. Begin to unfold your left leg directly to the ground to step forward on to the ball of your left foot to repeat. Now keep going. (When you are able to do this by yourself, try it with a partner, holding him or her around the back of the waist with your inside arm.)

Révérence

This will consist of rather grand, slow and quick walks taken from the dance.

3 When you have done six hop steps, leave out the last hop and stamp three times, knees bent and travelling forwards on each stamp. Open your arm forwards and out a little on these stamps and look at your hand.

The position of your leg in the hop is the same as for the skips that you will have learned in the earlier grades, but UNLIKE those, which bounce, hop steps move along the surface of the ground as if you were dancing under a low ceiling, with equal emphasis given to each movement.

Grade Four

The music is becoming more and more sophisticated, requiring more of a sense of performance as you continue to learn and develop your classical vocabulary.

AT THE BARRE

Pliés

This is a similar sequence to the one you learned in Grade Three, but it uses an arm movement on *demi-plié* and the simple *ports de bras* occur this time between the half and full movements. There is a rise at the end to check your balance.

Battements Tendus

These are a combination of *tendus en croix*, with and without the use of your arm.

Battements Glissés

These are still in two counts but with *three glissés* to each position *en croix*.

Ronds de Jambe

These are faster than Grade Three (two counts only) and start from a *dégagé* to 2nd position, where each one will finish.

Battements Fondus à Terre

These are a development from the previous grade. Stand sideways to the *barre*, feet in 3rd position and arm *bras bas*.

1 *Fondu* as before, releasing the front foot to *cou-de-pied*.

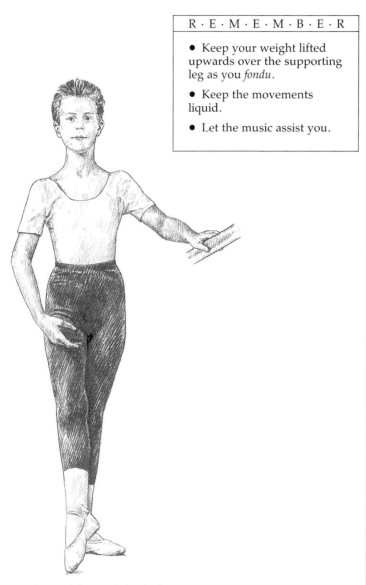

Grands Battements

These are divided into two movements only. From the throwing action, the leg descends directly to 3rd position, passing through the point on the ground in order to control the closing. Taken *en croix*.

2 As you lift out of the *fondu*, unfold your front leg *devant* with your toes lightly resting on the ground.

Repeat the *fondu*, bringing your pointed foot back to the *cou-de-pied* before extending it *à la seconde*. To give the supporting leg a rest, draw the extended one in to 3rd position *derrière*, at the same time rising on to the *demi-pointes*. Lower your heels. Now try it all in reverse – *derrière* then *à la seconde*.

AT THE BARRE

Développé à la Seconde

The *développé devant* has become faster, but as you are learning the movement *à la seconde* for the first time, face the *barre* and take it slowly as in Grade Three. Start in 1st position.

1 Slide the working foot up the *side* of the supporting leg in order not to lose the turnout in the thigh (where have you done this before?) The height of your foot will depend upon where you can hold your thigh as your leg unfolds. In this grade, your leg is not expected to extend higher than 45 degrees from the ground, so your foot will probably lift to the base of your calf only.

2 Keeping your thigh still and your hips square to the *barre*, unfold your leg to 2nd position, then lower it gradually to the ground and close *derrière* to 3rd position. Be careful not to lose any turnout in your thigh on the way down. In Grade Four, *développé* is combined with a practice at raising the leg to the back, stretched, to 45 degrees in preparation for an *arabesque en l'air* (in the air). You will meet it again in the centre, so occasionally take your hands off the *barre* to test your balance.

Relevés Passés Devant and Derrière

In the last grade, the *relevé* was taken on to two feet before separating one foot from the other, leaving you on one leg. Now you

RELEVÉ FROM TWO FEET TO ONE
1 *Relevé* on to your back foot, snatching it under you as before, and lift your front thigh smartly to place your foot under your knee as before.

are going to bypass the two feet and go directly to one. Start facing the *barre* with your feet in 3rd position.

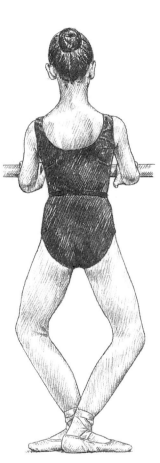

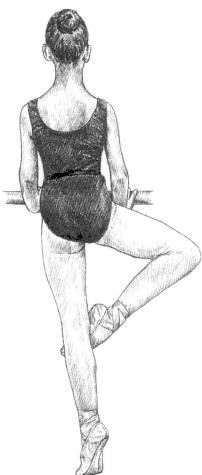

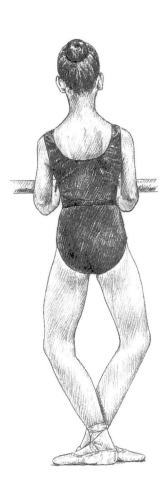

PASSÉ DERRIÈRE
2 With a slight spring, lower your raised foot to 3rd position *derrière* in *demi-plié*.

PASSÉ DEVANT
3 *Relevé* on to the same leg, this time lifting your back foot directly to the position under the knee at the *front* of the supporting leg. (Placing the foot to the front again helps to pin the working knee sideways, thus making it secure.) If the foot has taken the shortest, most direct journey there, an observer should not be able to detect the path that it has made from *plié* to knee.

4 Close the raised foot to 3rd position *devant* with a slight spring, finishing in *demi-plié*.

IN THE CENTRE

As usual, this starts with a relaxation exercise, using circling movements of the arms, which will assist in exercising and opening out the line across the shoulders and upper body.

Ports de Bras

This is a formal introduction to the arm-line of a 3rd *arabesque*. Look back at the last chapter to remind yourself of this *arabesque*.

Battements Tendus in Alignment

'Alignment' in this case means bringing your body into line on the *battement tendu devant* in the directions that you learned in Grade One, in sequence, starting *en croisé*, coming *en face*, changing *en ouvert*, before executing a *battement tendu* for the first time *en ecarté*. It needs control in the back and supporting leg. Look back in the book to remind yourself of those directions.

Pirouette en Dehors

This is a development from the previous grade. Start in 3rd position *en face* with your hands firmly on your waist, elbows to the side.

Boys and girls have a different preparation but the *relevé* and head action remains the same for both.

1 *Relevé devant* making a quarter turn to the right. When you travel away from the supporting leg like this, the *pirouette* is said to be travelling round *en dehors* (outwards). Leave your head behind, looking to the front.

> ### R·E·M·E·M·B·E·R
>
> • Keep your posture firm with the help of your hands on your waist on the quarter-turn.
>
> • Keep the sides of your neck of equal length so your head does not tilt as your body leaves it behind.

2 Spring your foot to 3rd position *derrière* (*devant* for the girls) in *demi-plié*, holding your head where it is on the close. Repeat all this three times, bringing your head erect on the next *relevé* and turning a quarter to your right each time, until you arrive back *en face*. In the girls' version make the last *relevé passé derrière* so the turns can repeat to the other side.

Exercise for Pirouette en Dedans

This *pirouette* is going to turn inwards towards the supporting leg, *en dedans*. Start *en face* in 3rd position, arms *bras bas*.

1 *Dégagé* the front foot *devant*, arms in 1st position.

2 Transfer the weight to the front leg *en fondu*, arms in 3rd position.

3 Releasing the back heel, push off the back leg into a *relevé passé devant*. Your side arm is swiftly going to join your front arm in a slightly shrunken 1st position, to keep both arms compact with your body. Stay there for a moment before springing your front foot to 3rd position *devant* in *demi-plié*, then recover. Remember on the *relevé* to *pirouette* position to lift the lower part of your back over your leg or you will not be able to balance there. It is harder to do from a *fondu*!

Practise on the other leg and then you are going to try your first turn!

IN THE CENTRE

The Turn

1 Start as before and, as you *relevé*, pull your body upwards and simultaneously round to the right, with your shoulders and hips moving in one piece. (Don't pull too hard for a single turn.) Leave your head and eyes behind, as for *pirouette en dehors*, until you can no longer see the front.

R·E·M·E·M·B·E·R

- Lift your body well on top of the supporting leg.

- Relax your shoulders.

- Brace the working knee to the side – it will be tempted to fall forwards.

- Keep your head straight as you turn away from the front.

2 Continue turning, whipping your head to the right in advance of your body and focusing your eyes immediately you can see the front again. Try to find something specific to look at, which makes it easier.

Now try it the other way round, so the *pirouette* turns to the left. From time to time practise more than one turn. If you fall over, pick yourself up, dust yourself down and start all over again.

Pas de Bourrées (under)

This means 'step of the *bourrée*', an eighteenth-century dance. It involves running steps and there are more than 28 varieties but don't worry – we are only going to study one here. *Pas de bourrées* are a very important part of a dancer's vocabulary. They can be used in a series, to give speed and neatness to the footwork, and they can be

1 Extend your back (right) foot to 2nd *en fondu*, arms *bras bas*, at the end of the introductory music.

used as linking steps in *enchaînements*. They can also be used as a spring-board, leading to big jumps. To add to their versatility, they can also be taken turning and on full point. Good use of the legs and feet and a well-poised body are essential if lightness and speed are to be

achieved. Practice the *pas de bourrées* slowly until you can do them correctly. Then gradually increase your speed until you are able to skim along the floor without losing speed and accuracy. Start *en face* with your right foot in 3rd position *derrière*, ready to travel to the left.

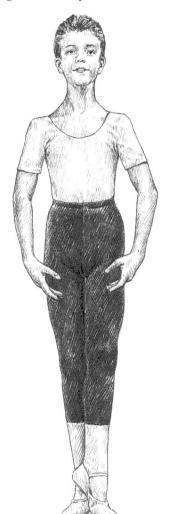

2 Draw your right leg back into 3rd position *derrière*, rising on to *demi-pointe*.

3 Step to 2nd position with your left foot.

4 Lower gently into *demi-plié* as you draw your right foot into 3rd position *devant*, head turned towards your front foot. Extend your back (left) foot to 2nd position to repeat it all travelling to the right. (Say to yourself 'behind, side, front'.)

IN THE CENTRE

Glissades (derrière and devant)

This is another new step and one
that glides close to the ground.
Like *pas de bourrées* it can serve
either as a preparation for big
springs (*grand allegro*) or as a link
from one step to another. Start
with your right foot in 3rd position
derrière, arms *bras bas*, ready to
travel to the right.

DERRIÈRE
1 *Demi-plié*, then slide your right
foot out with a *glissé* action to 2nd
position.

2 Push firmly off your left leg,
sending your leading foot a little
further along the floor and lifting
yourself slightly into the air until
both feet are stretched. Leave your
head to the left a little, over your
front foot.

R·E·M·E·M·B·E·R

● Make good use of your legs and feet to create the lift in the middle.

● Keep both knees pressed out to the side – no allowing them to get friendly!

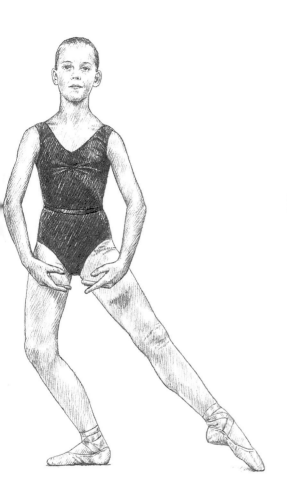

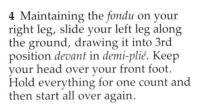

3 Transfer your weight over your right leg, lowering to a *fondu* and leaving your left leg fully stretched. Do not move your head. So far, does this remind you of another step in a previous grade?

4 Maintaining the *fondu* on your right leg, slide your left leg along the ground, drawing it into 3rd position *devant* in *demi-plié*. Keep your head over your front foot. Hold everything for one count and then start all over again.

Do two *glissades* with a hold in between and then try one followed immediately by a *changement*, stretch bend. Now repeat it to the left, beginning with your left foot.

Repeat it all starting with your front foot (*glissade devant*).

IN THE CENTRE

Balancés en Avant and en Arrière

En avant means travelling forwards and *en arrière* means travelling backwards, so this step is going to rock forwards and backwards.

Start *en croisé* and get ready to use your back foot, arms *demi-seconde* for the girls and *bras bas* for the boys.

EN AVANT
1 Take a good step forwards with your back foot in an *ouvert* direction, moving your arms through *bras bas* to 1st and on to 1st *arabesque*. *Balancé* as for *de côté*, closing your second foot in behind and looking out over your fingertips.

EN ARRIÈRE
2 Step backwards using your back foot, still in *ouvert*, beginning to lower your front arm to 3rd position and leaning forward a little from your waist. Look over your front arm.

3 Pass your front foot behind your back one, so the lilting part is in a *croisé* direction. Now you are ready to begin again.

These *balancés* will be combined in this grade with a *temps levé* in 1st *arabesque* so the whole sequence travels *en diagonale*, with or without changing direction.

IN THE CENTRE

Assemblés (over)

Assemblé means 'assembled' or 'brought together' and refers to the fact that, having taken off into the air from one leg, your feet are drawn together ('assembled') in the air before alighting on two legs. An *assemblé* can also be linked to other steps, particularly *glissades* which act as a good preparatory movement to help your body high into the air. Start in 3rd position, right foot *derrière* and arms *bras bas*.

Assemblé will be combined with a simple springing step (*soubresaut*) which will isolate the clinging of one foot to the other in the air. You will already have learned and practised *soubresauts* in previous grades.

1 As usual before a spring, begin with a *demi-plié*, then *battement glissé* to 2nd with your back (right) foot, beginning to push upwards from the *fondu* towards the end. Start to open your arms sideways.

2 Helped by the force of the extension, spring high into the air, fully stretching the underneath foot and lifting your arms to *demi-seconde*. If you are brave you can turn your head towards the outstretched foot!

R·E·M·E·M·B·E·R

● Spring as high as the music will allow to give you time to assemble your feet BEFORE you alight.

● Keep your posture particularly well supported to help your spring.

● Control your arms – they may try to help you too much.

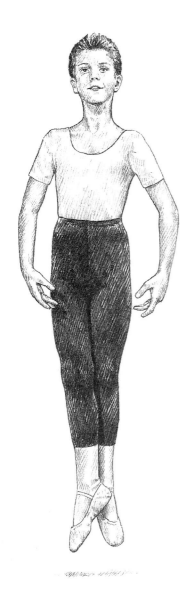

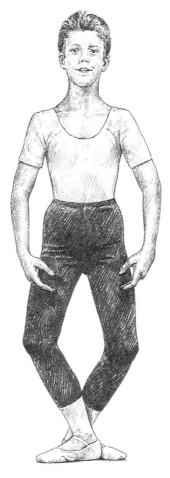

3 While in the air (if possible) pull your right leg in over your left, drawing one foot in front of the other (the *assemblé*).

4 Lower through your legs and feet into *demi-plié* in 3rd position. Stretch your knees and then *demi-plié* to repeat it with your other foot.

IN THE CENTRE

Flying Hops

This is another step from the Free Movement section, and travels in an anti-clockwise circle. It is a liberating step and you may enjoy using it to develop a sense of elevation. Try it without shoes and tights so you can feel your foot pushing into the ground to lift you up.

The technique of the step will already have been established in Grade Two, but let us recapitulate for a moment. Start feet together, arms relaxed at your sides, with your right foot relaxed and ready to go.

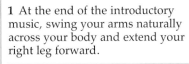

1 At the end of the introductory music, swing your arms naturally across your body and extend your right leg forward.

R·E·M·E·M·B·E·R

- Not to shorten your back by lifting your back leg and arms too high.

- Travel well and with equal distance on the two runs forwards.

- Do not rise too high on these runs or you will cut down the distance travelled and make yourself pop up like a champagne cork!

2 Step forward on your right leg, swinging your arms outwards and upwards into a high V-shape, head poised as you learned in Grade One. Hop in that position with your back leg held low, not turned out as for your Classical work but nevertheless extended fully right down to the tips of your toes. Now, instead of stepping backwards, as in Grade Two, keep your weight over your leg and carry on with two quick steps forwards, low down on the ball of your foot, swinging your arms in and across your body under their own weight, and relaxing your upper back and head before repeating the whole sequence on the other foot.

RHYTHM AND

These are still in Russia, but the rhythm steps introduce syncopation, the displacing of accents, making some movements stronger and others weak.

1 Rock on to the ball of your left foot and the heel of your right foot, with your weight sitting equally between the two. Rock the other way, reversing your feet. Repeat it all again (four rocks in all).

R·E·M·E·M·B·E·R

- Keep your body upright and between your feet on the rocking steps.

- Ease your knees when travelling.

- Keep the snake step oily and smooth.

CHARACTER STEPS

Snake Step

Start in 1st position *en face*, girls holding their skirt with their left hand, right fist on their hip. Boys, you rest your right fist on your left elbow, with your left fist under your right elbow – rather like arms folded, but without the fold.

Révérence

After the dance, the *révérence* will combine Hop Steps with stamps before turning to thank the teacher and the pianist.

2 Travelling to the right and, keeping your knees slightly relaxed, swivel your right foot inwards on the BALL of the foot, lowering your heel, and your left foot inwards on the HEEL, lowering the toes. Look to the right. It is important to make sure that your feet are equally turned.

3 Still travelling and looking to the right, turn your right foot out on the HEEL, lowering your toes, and your left foot out on the BALL of the foot, lowering your heel, ending with the feet equally turned. Do the 'in' and 'out' movements again as described, keeping the movement smooth as if you were moving along a rail, rather than bobbing up and down.

Now start it all again, beginning the rocking to the right if you are going to travel the snake step to the left. Of course, girls should change the hand holding their skirt and boys should put the other arm on top.

With a partner, start side by side and rock towards each other first to travel away on the snake step, then reverse it all, travelling towards your partner.

Grade Five

Grade Five is the culmination of much study and hard work. The way in which the exercises and steps have been combined in this grade should encourage you to demonstrate the technical skills that you have acquired, along with a heightened sense of rhythm and musicality, well co-ordinated movement and, most important of all, your love of dancing.

AT THE BARRE

The 3rd position of the feet becomes 5th position, requiring a correct and fully supported posture, if a sufficiently equal turnout of the legs is to be achieved.

Pliés

Now, at last, *pliés* are taken like a professional dancer with one hand resting on the *barre*, slightly in front of the body with the elbow relaxed but not bent. The other arm is going to assist the full *plié* with the simple *ports de bras* that you have been practising in the previous two grades. This begins in 2nd position of the arms and, on

1 Sink slowly through a *demi-plié*, beginning to lower your arm.

2 By the time you have reached the depth of the *grand plié* your arm will be in *bras bas*.

the downward movement, descends slowly to *bras bas*. On the way up, it passes through 1st position on the recovery to *demi-plié* and when you have fully stretched the knees it will be back in 2nd position. If you time it well it will look co-ordinated. Begin in 1st position with your arm in 2nd.

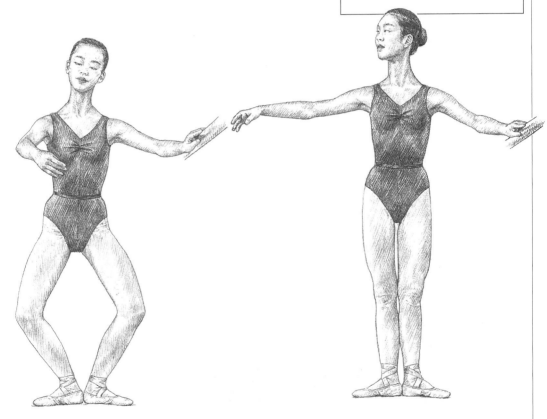

3 Slowly recover through *demi-plié*, raising your arm to 1st position.

4 Finally brace your knees and thighs while fully opening your arm to 2nd position.

The exercise is combined with *demi-pliés* in 1st, 2nd and 5th positions, with a slow, controlled rise at the end.

AT THE BARRE

Battements Tendus with Transfer of Weight

In this grade you are going to add a transfer of weight with *demi-plié* to 4th position opposite 5th. Start in 5th position, arms *bras bas*.

Battements Glissés

Adds a *petit retiré*.

Battements Fondus

Combined now with *ronds de jambe à terre*.

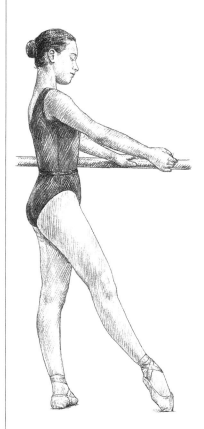

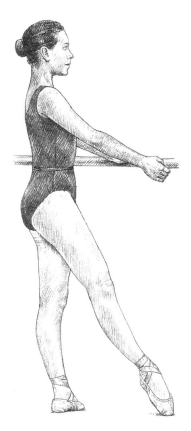

1 *Dégagé devant* with your arm to 1st, looking into your hand.

2 Lower into a *demi-plié* in 4th position, head erect, transferring your weight evenly between your legs.

3 *Dégagé devant*, transferring all your weight back on to your supporting leg, closing firmly to 5th position. Continue *en croix*, opening and holding your arm to 2nd position.

Exercise for Battements Frappés

This is a new exercise so where will it face? That's right, the *barre*. *Frappé* means 'beaten' or 'struck' and in its final form the ball of your foot will strike the surface of the floor. However, the exercise here is preparatory and is intended to teach you the action of the knee and ankle only. It will help you to develop quick footwork for steps in the centre.

R · E · M · E · M · B · E · R

● Extend your leg firmly but not so hard that it jars the knee joint. It isn't good for it!

● Keep your thigh still in 2nd position throughout. Try not to let it rise up and down.

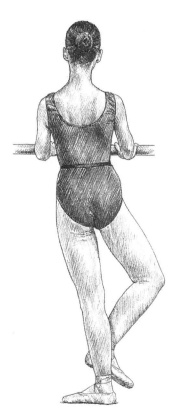

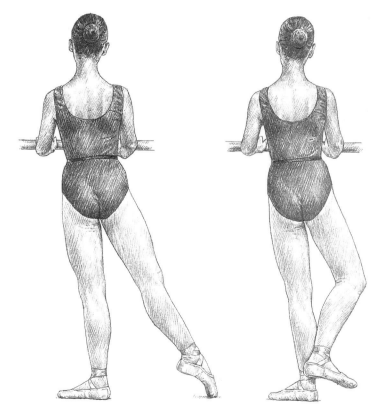

1 The position that your working foot begins from is *cou-de-pied* with a flexed foot.

2 Keeping your thigh still, extend your lower leg by stretching your knee, ankle and toes to 2nd position.

3 Now fold your working leg in from your knee so your foot is flexed and placed in *cou-de-pied derrière*.

AT THE BARRE

Fouetté of Adage

The *développé devant* is combined with *développé à la seconde* and includes this new movement, which will re-appear in the centre where the slow, controlled and unsupported exercises (*adage*) are performed.

1 Start from a *dégagé* to 2nd position, sideways to the *barre*, arm in 2nd.

2 Raise your supporting heel a little off the ground and, swivelling on the ball of your foot, push your heel forward a few inches, beginning to bring the far side of your body towards the *barre* with your arm, while retaining your working leg in 2nd position.

3 Repeat this pivot on your supporting leg, moving further round towards the *barre*, carrying your arm round with your shoulder. Move your hip and shoulder in one piece. Your working leg will now reluctantly begin to rotate inwards.

4 The final pivot (number 3) will bring your body square to the *barre*, both arms placed upon it and with your working leg now extended behind your hip in an *arabesque* line.

AT THE BARRE

Développés Derrière

On this occasion the working foot is going to begin in 5th position *devant* and will pass through *retiré* to the back. Although it is a new movement it will start sideways to the *barre*, as the exercise involves other movements, including a *chassé*.

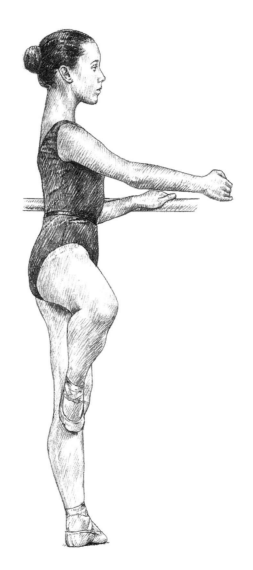

1 Draw your foot up the front of your leg, raising your arm to 1st position, until it reaches a low *retiré* at the side.

2 Holding your thigh at the same height, slowly push it backwards as your leg unfolds so that by the time your knee has straightened your leg will be directly behind your hip. Unlike *développé devant*, your thigh begins to move backwards BEFORE the unfolding of the lower half of your leg, in order to keep the turnout already established in the hip joint. Lower your leg and close as before. (Note that your body tilts forward as in *grands battements derrière*.)

AT THE BARRE

Chassé and Rotation

This is attached to the previous exercise. *Chassé* means 'chased' or 'hunted' and, although it has not been discussed in this book until now, you will have encountered it before in the *développé* exercise in Grade Four. Start in 5th position in *demi-plié*, arm *bras bas*.

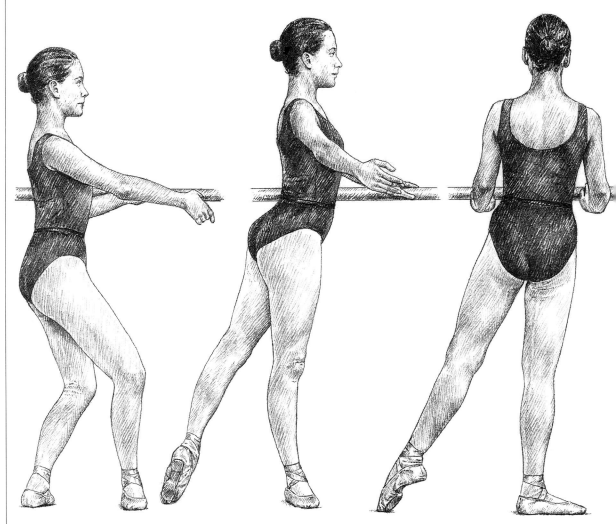

CHASSÉ

1 Remaining at the depth of the *demi-plié*, push your front foot forwards, transferring your weight between your legs (like the *tendu* exercise with transfer of weight) and raising your arm to 1st position.

2 Continue to travel forwards and upwards, pushing up off your back leg until your weight is fully transferred over the front one, opening your arm to 2nd position.

ROTATION

3 Begin to rotate your back thigh outwards, drawing your body round to the *barre* with two pivoting actions on your supporting leg (like *fouetté* in reverse). Carry your arm round to the *barre* with the shoulder.

R·E·M·E·M·B·E·R

● In *chassé* carry the weight of your body forwards with your leg.

● In rotation, only raise your heel as much as it needs to skim the floor, holding the turnout firmly in the thigh of your supporting leg.

Grands Battements

Combined with a *retiré passé*.

Exercise for Pirouette en Dehors

The *barre* ends with an exercise to assist with the turning of a *pirouette en dehors*.

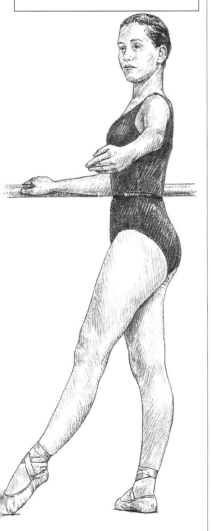

4 Continue to rotate your working leg outwards, drawing your body round to the other side with two further pivots. Your working leg will now have rotated from *dégagé derrière*, through 2nd position to, with a little adjustment of the leg, *dégagé devant*!

IN THE CENTRE

In the relaxation exercise your arms swing in unison from one side of your body to the other. This is a particularly useful preparation for the boys' step in the Free Movement section later on.

Ports de Bras

This is a sophisticated and elegant combination of *chassés* and transfer of weight into different positions of the arms.

Battements Tendus

This is a combination of *battements tendus devant* with a transfer of weight forwards.

Adage Study

This is an amalgamation of *chassés*, *développés* and the *fouetté* movement learned at the *barre*, finishing in a 1st *arabesque en l'air*!

Pirouette en Dehors

With a full turn right and left!

Pirouette en Dedans

This is the Grade Four exercise, made more difficult by beginning *en croisé*, instead of *en face*.

Glissades (over and under)

These are the same as Grade Four, except with a change of foot each time. When the commencing foot starts at the back in 5th position and finishes at the front, the *glissade* is said to be 'over'. Similarly, when the commencing foot starts at the front and finishes at the back, it is called 'under'.

Balancés

This is a combination of all the other *balancés* that you have learned with a *balancé* turning.

IN THE CENTRE

Exercise for Tour en L'air

BOYS

If you go to the ballet, you will see the male dancers executing this step. It is often used to finish off a solo dance with bravura. Here is the preparatory exercise to assist the placing of the body and legs in the air while turning. Start in 5th position, right foot *devant*, arms *bras bas*.

R·E·M·E·M·B·E·R

- Lift your body straight into the air.

- Control your arms.

- Keep your legs close together on the turn.

1 *Relevé* in 5th position, raising your arms directly to 3rd position.

2 Lower in *demi-plié*, holding your arms and back in place.

3 Spring, pulling your left arm round to join the other one in 1st position and changing your feet over with a quarter-turn in the air to the right, with your head and eyes remaining to the front. Alight in *demi-plié* in 5th position, arms in 1st, head still to the front.

IN THE CENTRE

Flying Hops

These are as for Grade Four but they change direction on the two runs. They need good focus and a sense of purpose.

Step and Hop with Body Turns

BOYS
This is a step from the Free Movement section normally only shown by the boys, but there is nothing to stop the girls having a go. Start with your feet together, right foot relaxed, arms hanging naturally at your sides, ready to travel in an anti-clockwise circle.

1 Swinging both arms forwards, prepare to step out on your right leg.

Studies

In this grade both boys and girls will have the choice of studying one of two Classical studies or a Free Movement study.

2 Now hop high into the air on your right leg, drawing your left foot swiftly to a skipping position and pulling both arms down and back with a strong turn of your body to the left. Follow your arms with your head and clench your hands, like a matador taunting the bull with his cape.

Follow this with two runs to repeat on the other side.

R · E · M · E · M · B · E · R

- Step out well.

- Swing your arms across with vigour on the hop.

- Lift your head and body well into the air.

RHYTHM AND CHARACTER STEPS

The Polish Court style has been chosen for this grade and, as for your other sections, it should look sophisticated and elegant, with a controlled ease of movement. If you have been fortunate enough to see the classical ballets of the nineteenth century at the theatre, you will readily identify this style of Character dancing.

The position of the hands is clenched on the hips, as for the two previous grades, with the elbows slightly forward of the body, if this can be achieved without closing up the shoulders.

Holubetz

This can be done in 2/4 or 3/4 rhythm, the latter being the easier of the two. Your set step will begin with a spring from 1st position (the Polish style makes more use of turnout than the other two styles), but here it is described as starting with a step across, as it is easier to learn that way.

R·E·M·E·M·B·E·R

- Keep your leg turned out as you step across.

- Do not release your right leg too high or the left one will never catch it up to click heels!

- Turn your lower arm with graceful ease from the elbow NOT the wrist.

TRAVELLING TO THE RIGHT
1 From 1st position, step across your body on your left foot (turned out), lowering your head and eyes a little and releasing your left arm to an upward open line, the arm turned at the elbow so the palm faces down.

2 Release your right leg to the side (low).

3 Spring into the air, drawing the underneath (left) leg up to the right one to click heels (known as a *cabriole*). On the click, lift your head and eyes sharply and roll your lower arm inwards from the elbow to create a curve with the palm up. If this sounds difficult, it is, because the click and the head movement are both sharp, while the arm movement remains oily!

Going on to the Higher Grades

Now you are well on your way to the higher grades (Six, Seven and Eight). You will have learned most of the vocabulary needed for these by now and the higher grades will, therefore, concentrate on teaching you style, in particular, that of the Romantic ballets from the early to mid-nineteenth century. They will also demonstrate how to move about your imaginary stage, using many floor patterns, without stumbling into other people. The Free Movement will train you to involve your body fully, using a long, billowing silk scarf, and you will continue to become more fully conversant with sophisticated and theatrical Character styles.

Having come this far, continue to have fun!

4 Alight on your left leg, right leg released, holding your head and arm still.

5 Continue to deepen the *fondu*, then step out well on to your right leg.

6 Step across your body, lowering your head and eyes and rolling your lower arm outwards from the elbow, ready to *cabriole* once more.

This step can also travel to the left and can be done with a partner, either travelling towards and away from each other or turning in a circle holding on to each other round the waist.

I WAS ABOUT THREE YEARS old when my mother realized that dancing lessons would be the best thing for me. We lived in a little village in Dorset and whenever my parents' friends came over I'd insist on entertaining them by jumping up and down on the sofa. So I started having lessons at the local ballet school in Sherborne and then went to the Dorchester Ballet Club. When I was ten, we had to move up to Chester because of my father's business. I was offered a place at the Hammond School, even though I was a year younger than my classmates. Boarding was awful at first and our routine at the Hammond was very disciplined: at the age of ten we were expected to do our own washing and ironing. At weekends everyone would go home, but because my parents lived four hours away from the school, I could only go home at half-term and during the holidays.

By the time I reached thirteen or fourteen I decided to concentrate more on ballet. I was about to do my GCSEs (a year early) and I'd got honours in my RAD Elementary and come first in my assessments. It was then that I thought perhaps I should concentrate on ballet. So at fourteen I auditioned at White Lodge, was accepted, and joined the third-year class in order to put me back with my own age group. It was very hard work at first because the whole approach to ballet there was quite different to what I'd been used to at Hammond. Everyone knew who was who in the Royal Ballet Company. I remember my first visit to Covent Garden with the school; we saw Sylvie Guillem dancing in *Cinderella*. I loved it. Before that I'd only seen the Bolshoi.

At sixteen, I gained a place at the Upper School and moved to London. Like most first-year girls, I share a room in Wolf House, which is very near school. We have a landlady to keep an eye on us, but as long as you stick to a few

A DAY IN THE LIFE OF
NICOLE TONGUE
Student at the Royal Ballet School

rules – such as the 11 p.m. curfew – you're a free person. At the Upper School, the first ballet class starts at 8.30 a.m., which is quite early enough for me. I let my room-mates drag me out of bed because I'm not very good at getting up in the mornings. I do my hair in bed, with my eyes closed. Then I put on a clean leotard and tights and have some breakfast – a bowl of cereal and two pieces of toast or, if it's getting late, yoghurt and some fruit. At the beginning of term I made myself get up at 7 a.m. so that I could have an hour and a half to get myself properly organized, but as the term progressed I began to feel more and more exhausted. Now I get up at 7.30 a.m. and it's a mad rush to reach the studio by 8 a.m. so that I can have a proper warm-up before class. Once there, I put on my woolly and my ballet shoes and do some body conditioning and stretching exercises.

Class lasts for an hour and a half – which I much prefer to the two-hour classes we used to have at White Lodge – and each day it's different, so you can't just fall asleep and go through the motions. It's a very good form of mental stimulation first thing in the morning. We're doing much harder work than at White Lodge, but we're also given more of a chance to dance in class. At White Lodge it was all quite technical: you concentrated a lot on *placement*. Here you're left to your own devices, but guided along the way. There's more room for individuality, for your own interpretation.

Each day, after ballet class, I have a one-hour lesson in one of my A level subjects. I've always been very conscientious about my academic work. Being a year younger than my classmates at Hammond, I had to push myself that bit harder. At White Lodge, I did seven GCSEs (I got six A grades and one B) and now I'm doing two A levels: Dance and English Literature and Language. We also do contextual studies at the school, including sociology, art and music appreciation.

Although everyone has a different timetable, we tend to meet up in the canteen at lunchtime. Depending on how short of money I am, I either make my own sandwiches or I buy some in the canteen. Sometimes I have pasta instead, and maybe some yoghurt or an apple. I find it quite difficult to have a hot meal during the day, so I usually leave my main meal until the evening. And I take calcium tablets because I don't drink much milk.

Each week we have a contemporary class and sessions specifically for *pas de deux* and solos. We also have a repertoire class twice a week in which we learn *corps de ballet* work. Then there's choreography. If, like me, you're interested in it, you're encouraged to make dance pieces and to enter the school's choreography competition for the Ursula Moreton Award.

The day finishes at around 5.30 p.m. Sometimes I try to arrange a choreographic rehearsal after school and everyone moans and groans. But that's the only time available, apart from Saturday afternoons. On Monday evenings I usually go to a supermarket in Hammersmith to do my food shopping, I'm very strict about eating well, making sure I have plenty of fish, chicken, vegetables and salads. It's so easy just to have a tin of soup or something that's not very nutritious.

Some evenings I go to the theatre or to a dance performance. The school gives out a number of free standing passes for Royal Ballet performances, so there's always a mad rush to get your name up on the board. So far I've seen *Mayerling* and *Swan Lake*. But I also like West End musicals, fringe theatre and contemporary dance. I think it's important to look at all styles of dance and find out what the body can do, especially if you want to learn more about choreography. On the nights when I don't go out, I tend to collapse in a heap on my bed and watch whatever's on the television before falling asleep for an hour or so. Then I'll make something to eat, have a shower and get on with A level work and essays. I try to be in bed by 11 each night at the latest.

In general, I'm a confident, happy person, but on days when everything's been a disaster and I feel I can't cope I'll phone my mother and cry my eyes out. She's very good at picking up the pieces and putting them back together again. Being injured is one of the most depressing things imaginable for a dancer but you've just got to deal with it. And sometimes a teacher may scream her head off at you, but it's only because she wants more out of you. My parents are a great support and would stand by me in whatever career I'd chosen. They were very proud when Peter Wright chose me to dance Clara in *The Nutcracker* in 1990. Unfortunately, the night my mother brought all her friends along to see it, everything went wrong: the scenery got ripped, the sleigh broke down . . .

I'm nearly seventeen so it's not long before I'll have to go out and find a job – and I won't find one at the local Job Centre. Naturally, I hope to get into the Royal Ballet or Birmingham Royal Ballet, but if that didn't happen I'd look abroad. I think it's very important to keep an open mind, never to believe that this is the only place to be, the only thing to be doing, because you can't predict what will happen. Dancing is a very risky business but, deep down, I know I want a career in ballet and, eventually, to become a Principal. At present, the dancers who most inspire me are Viviana Durante, Lesley Collier, Fiona Chadwick and Deborah Bull, but I do think that certain dancers suit particular ballets. Maybe I'm not as technically amazing as some dancers, but I do love performing. Whenever I've had the chance to be on stage, I've always felt certain it was the right place for me to be.

I FIRST BECAME involved with dancing when I was about eight years old. My early experience was fairly typical, I guess. I used to round up a few of my neighbours and cousins, and my older brother Mark, and choreograph routines to my favourite music. At the end of the day, all the parents would be invited to watch these epic backyard productions! I was nearly always centre front, of course!

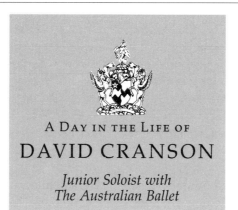

A DAY IN THE LIFE OF

DAVID CRANSON

*Junior Soloist with
The Australian Ballet*

My parents have always been very supportive. Basically they wanted me to do whatever made me happy. Eventually they took me to a theatre school that taught various kinds of dancing as well as singing and drama. There was a group attached to the school called The Young Company and we performed in variety shows in clubs and on television. I also did some commercials and modelling.

After about three years, two of my teachers advised me that if I wanted to be a good dancer, I needed classical ballet training. This was the last thing I thought I needed, but we took their advice anyway and looked in the local area for a ballet school. We found the Ann McDonald School of Dancing in Enfield, a suburb of Sydney, and I started there in 1982.

My passion for classical ballet grew so quickly that within six months I had decided that this was what I wanted. It was so different, so intense, and such a challenge! In 1984 I took my first RAD examination (Senior Grade) and got Honours. The year after that, Margaret Markham, one of the Directors of the school, established a vocational day school where students could train in ballet as well as undertake their academic studies. This was the perfect way to get more dancing into my day and so I became one of the first students at the new McDonald College. That year I got Highly Commended for my Elementary examination and was cast in the first of several roles which I had the chance to

perform each year at the school's performance.

These performances were produced very professionally by Anne Fraser, who had been a soloist with The Australian Ballet before joining the school's teaching staff. We all had to audition for the roles and rehearsals went on all year before the big occasion at the Sydney Opera House in December. Sometimes we had guest artists from The Australian Ballet to dance with us, which was very exciting.

Miss Fraser treated me very sympathetically. I think she felt that if I was pushed the wrong way I would just give up. She encouraged me but she was always realistic. I'll never forget her saying to me, as she offered me my role for that year's performance, 'If you work at this, you might . . .?' Eventually I got to do Blue Boy in *Les Patineurs* and Blue Bird from *Sleeping Beauty* among several other roles.

John Byrne, who is now Artistic Director of the Royal Academy of Dancing, was also on the staff of the College at that time. He taught me a lot over the next three years before he left towards the end of 1987 to train as a Major Examiner in London. I was very lucky to have had such a wonderful and understanding teaching faculty. I must admit that I was not the easiest of students. Actually, I was probably the loudest, most obnoxious and undisciplined of students with an ego to match. Far from being an angel!

In 1987 I stopped doing my academic subjects and became a full-time ballet student. During the year I began to have doubts about whether ballet was the right career choice for me. I went through a bad, uncertain period but I finally realized that other career ambitions could wait; a dancing career had to be started young and, if I didn't try, I would always regret it.

Later that year I auditioned for the Australian Ballet School and was accepted. At the audition

I met Betsy Sawers, a well-known and respected teacher in Australia. Betsy had taught several Advanced boys and she invited me down to her school in Canberra for extra coaching just before my examination. She was very generous to me and her intensive coaching gave me confidence. I got Honours and I was off to take part in the Genée competition in London!

I was the only male candidate that year which was a bit difficult, but I expected nonetheless to get into the finals. I can still remember the shock when I didn't make it. Once again I asked the question: was it worth it? On the way home I re-ran the whole week in my mind – what if I'd done this differently, what if . . . ? But, really, I just wasn't ready. I moved to Melbourne and started work at the Australian Ballet School with a clear idea of what I needed to do.

My first teacher was Robert Ray. He based a lot of our work on the Vaganova method which is so strengthening. He was very thorough and hard to please but we all improved a lot. I worked harder than ever before and topped the year. The late Kelvin Coe, a former First Principal with the Company, took us in the second year. His demonstration was beautiful to watch and he encouraged us all to develop a highly professional approach to our work.

During my second year I decided to try and get my Solo Seal. The school was not then very happy to coach anyone for examination work so I found a small ballet school, the Karen Stephens Academy, around the corner from where I lived and went there three or four times a week. When the school found out I was nearly expelled. But I was determined to achieve my goal and I got so much from working with Miss Stephens. I also got my Seal! My sights were set again on the Genée. My confidence was given an extra boost when, just before I left for London, Maina Gielgud, Artistic Director of the Company, offered me a contract without my having to do a third year at the school.

It was so strange to go back to London again. At first, I felt a bit embarrassed, but I knew I was there for one thing only – to dance in the finals on stage at the Palladium and not to watch as I had two years before.

The week went so fast. I made it to the finals. Desmond Kelly took the class on stage. It was a lovely class and I enjoyed myself. I danced my variations and felt really happy with them. The girls' medals were announced. No gold. Then the boys. Gold only – to me! It was a night I'll never forget and it made all the effort I'd put in worthwhile.

Company life is so different to school. It's even more tiring, with longer hours, but you perform a lot more and that's what I love the most – showing to an audience the thing which means the most to you. Being able to express yourself in this way is wonderful. It's like having an extra set of senses.

In my first year in the company I danced the Drummer Boy in *Graduation Ball* and then my first Principal role as Franz in *Coppelia*. I felt a little unprepared for the pressure of a full-length role but it seemed to go all right and I learnt a lot from it. Since then I have danced quite a few soloist roles including Principal Boy in *Etudes*, Red Knight in *Checkmate* and the Peasant *pas de deux* in *Giselle*. I have also toured the USA and Europe and I was recently promoted to Coryphée (Junior Soloist).

I'm very happy most of the time. Like all dancers, I've had the down times when I've been off with stress fractures or having bone spurs removed from my ankles. Now that I've begun to establish my career I always try to leave some time for myself and I like to go out and meet people with different approaches and ideas. I love talking about anything that interests other people, but dancing is at the centre of my life. I'm very committed to it. At the moment I just want to dance forever – trying to attain my ultimate goals and loving it!

International Dancers

DARCEY BUSSELL
ROYAL BALLET

I STARTED BALLET CLASSES at my local ballet school on Saturday mornings when I was four. After prep school I went to a stage school to concentrate on the arts. I enjoyed the work and tried everything from tap dancing to singing but I realized after the first year that ballet was my favourite and that if I wanted to become accomplished in a particular field I would have to concentrate on this, and only this. I was very lucky to obtain a place at White Lodge, the Royal Ballet Junior School, and started there at the age of thirteen. I was behind in the ballet curriculum and had to work very hard to catch up with my peers. I was also stepping into a class made up of already established friendships. I think in retrospect that all this drove me harder to achieve my goal and to make something of the art I had chosen.

After White Lodge and graduating to the Upper School at Barons Court I was lucky to join Sadlers Wells Royal Ballet, now known as the Birmingham Royal Ballet. In the touring company I was able to perform solo roles and was able to gain experience quite quickly.

My career took off when Sir Kenneth Macmillan asked me to be Princess Rose in his three-act ballet *The Prince of the Pagodas*. So, at nineteen, I moved over to the Royal Ballet at the Royal Opera House in London. It was very sad leaving all my friends at Sadlers Wells, but I was going to a lovely company and was indeed lucky to have been part of such a supportive team. It was a great thrill to work with Sir Kenneth Macmillan. After performing the ballet on the first night Anthony Dowell made me a Principal of the Company. I was speechless!

So, at twenty, I was dancing Principal roles including *Swan Lake*, which I had always dreamed of doing. The only thing I would have loved is to have had more time to rehearse before performing my first *Swan Lake* – due to an injury I only had two weeks to rehearse in the studio. When on tour in Japan, I was asked to dance the role of Nikiya in *La Bayadere* when Sylvie Guillem injured herself. I had only three days to prepare before performing it and that was scary! I could not refuse the opportunity but would have liked three to four weeks to prepare for such a big role, but it was amazing to dance and I cannot wait to do it again. Often the best things happen this way.

However many times I dance a role I never get bored. Somehow there is always something new about it, something I did not discover before. There are so many old ballets to rediscover, new ballets being written, different styles of dance to try. As long as I am part of this and always busy I am happy. I have a lot to look forward to.

JOSEPH CIPOLLA
THE BIRMINGHAM ROYAL BALLET

I BEGAN STUDYING DANCE at seventeen – which is relatively late in life as dancers go – initially to gain an overall knowledge of dance before going to university to study musical theatre. I attended a course at the American Academy of Ballet and, because I showed talent, was advised to study with them rather than go to university and was offered a full scholarship. At the end of the course Karl Shook and Arthur Mitchell, co-directors of the Dance Theatre of Harlem who had both watched me dance, invited me to join the company's school. I was soon made an apprentice to the company and eventually a full company member. If it sounds as though this all happened very fast . . . it did! It seemed very lucky for someone who had started so late to be in the hands of such people as Karl Shook, a careful and patient teacher, and Arthur Mitchell, a generous man with a wealth of knowledge in the art of stage craft.

I had no choice but to learn very quickly and found that dancing was far more than *pliés* and *ports de bras*. The proper mental preparation was important, as was a positive attitude. This is still as important as ever because of the constant challenges presented by the classical repertoire of The Birmingham Royal Ballet. My experience in dancing the full-length classics was extremely limited before coming here and I can't help but think what a great risk Peter Wright was taking when he hired me. But I am thankful he did take the risk and would like to think it has paid off. I'll never call myself a ballet dancer, even after six years with The Birmingham Royal Ballet, a classical company. I prefer simply to be called a dancer. I learned an appreciation for all dance forms in those days with the Dance Theatre of Harlem and still find all types of dance exciting.

MIRANDA CONEY

THE AUSTRALIAN BALLET

Every time I hear music I have an irresistible urge to move. As a youngster I was constantly dancing around the living room performing for Mum and Dad whenever a record was on. I was fortunate in having a Mum with a very special love of dance and a talent for acting at what felt like the right moment. She learned ballet when she was younger and, recognizing that I would be at home in the world of dance, started me learning ballet with Diana Waldron's Perth City Ballet at the age of six. I was like a duck taking to water, and once I had a taste of theatrical life there was no turning back.

My years with Perth City Ballet were filled with opportunities. I thrived on the performing, the stage and the life of the theatre. For me it was sheer magic. I gave up many a school holiday and took part in endless festivals and concerts and was also encouraged to develop choreographic skills at a very young age, which I feel may be of value to me later in my career.

At eleven I joined Terri Charlesworth's Graduate College of Dance, which was a semi-professional group of about twelve students taking classes every day after school and all day Saturday. We visited Monte Carlo and had special training with Marika Besobrasova.

I joined The Australian Ballet School in 1982 and was accepted into the company halfway through my third year in 1984. Since then my promotion through the ranks has been a gradual one. I am now Principal with The Australian Ballet and loving the career I have chosen more than ever. There have been many highlights in my career to date, including my promotion to Principal in 1991 and first performance as such in *Swan Lake*, guesting with the Kirov Ballet in 1990, performing *Coppelia* for the Princess of Wales in London in 1992, being part of the Nureyev Gala and being in Graeme Murphy's new *The Nutcracker*.

The travel and touring to different parts of the world is also a very large part of being a performer. It is tiring but extremely rewarding and very confidence-boosting. During my eight years with the company I toured Japan and China in 1987, visited Russia, London and Athens in 1988, went to Singapore, Bangkok and Taiwan in 1989, New York, Washington and Costa Mesa in 1990, guested with the Kirov Ballet in *Giselle* and *La Sylphide* in 1990, and danced in London and Italy in 1992.

The life of a dancer is not an easy one. It requires immense discipline and dedication and enormous sacrifices in many areas. There is a ceaseless struggle to maintain good health, a good figure and looks, and a constant striving for perfection, but the rewards are many.

There is a certain personal satisfaction in achieving the goals we set ourselves. But, for me, there is no greater reward than in the realization that you have brought delight to all those who have watched you. For me this saying of Anna Pavlova says it all: 'A dancer must sacrifice herself to her art. Her reward will be the power to help those who come to see her forget awhile the sadness and monotony of life.'

STEVEN HEATHCOTE

THE AUSTRALIAN BALLET

I PROBABLY STARTED DANCING because of a childhood interest in movement in general. I was always very aware of how people moved with a particular gait, style or peculiarity. When I was four years old I saw a performance of *The Nutcracker* and was amazed and fascinated that these dancers could move like no one else I had ever seen. It was, I suppose, unique. That was the primary inspiration for me to start dance lessons at the age of ten. I had no real notion that I would take it to a professional level – it was just another activity along with my hockey, rugby and athletics. It wasn't until my early teens that I really started to know that I *had* to become a professional dancer. This was largely due to seeing The West Australian Ballet, The Australian Ballet and other international companies. Seeing artists such as Margot Fonteyn, Rudolph Nureyev, Kelvin Coe, Ross Stretton, Maya Plisetskaya, John Meehan, Marilyn Rowe and many other great dancers as well really kept my inspiration burning.

I suppose, to a degree, every child lives in a bit of a fantasy world, and seeing these wonderful story ballets, such as *Sleeping Beauty*, *Swan Lake*, *Carmen*, *Spartacus* and so on, only served to fuel my own fantasy.

When I was fifteen I auditioned for the Australian Ballet School, primarily for the ex-perience, so you can imagine the mixture of shock and delight on being told I had been accepted by the then Director, Dame Margaret Scott. It was followed two years later by more shock and delight when I was accepted into the main company by Marilyn Rowe.

My first year in the company was 1983 and this was the same year that Maina Gielgud took over the Directorship. After a few years my workload quickly increased and I found myself dancing most of the major roles within The Australian Ballet's repertoire. In 1987 I was promoted to Principal Artist. Since then I have been very fortunate to have guested with many overseas companies, including Ballet Nacional de Cuba, The Riga Ballet, Kiev Ballet, the Kirov Ballet and American Ballet Theatre.

Whether as a dancer or a coach I know that there will always be something more to discover about the elusive world of dance, and I hope to be able to continue to contribute to it for many years to come.

AMANDA McKERROW

AMERICAN BALLET THEATRE

I WAS FIVE YEARS OLD when I had my first experience of ballet. My mother used to take me along when she went to pick up my older sister from her ballet class, and I remember watching the end of class through the crack in the door. I loved it. I also wanted to do anything my sister did, so my mother enrolled me the following year. Right from the start I was hooked. It was definitely more difficult than it looked, but it made everything else I did seem somehow less important.

I began my training with the Royal Academy of Dance. It was an excellent foundation, and I found the exams a wonderful way to follow my progress. After that, I went to The Washington School of Ballet, where I became an apprentice with their company and later became a full company member. There I had the opportunity to work with different choreographers, and gained quite a bit of performing experience. When I joined American Ballet Theatre in 1982 I was very comfortable on stage.

I've been very fortunate in my career, and I've been able to do many different types of roles. There's no feeling for me quite like the one I get when I'm on stage. Time almost seems to stand still sometimes. Over the years I may have made many sacrifices for my career, but I can honestly say I wouldn't trade any of them. Ballet has given me the chance to travel all over the world, to meet many wonderful people – most importantly, my husband – and to be a part of one of the purest art forms of all.

BRUCE SANSOM

ROYAL BALLET

W HEN I WAS ASKED to write something about my dancing life I thought that rather than give a potted history of what, when and where, I would describe three events that are etched in my memory for their own distinct reasons.

In my final year at the Royal Ballet Upper School, the annual school performance was to include *Giselle*, a ballet which I had never seen. I took myself off to the Coliseum in London to watch the Festival Ballet (as it was called then) on two successive evenings. The first evening had Eva Evdokimova and Peter Schaufuss giving a dazzling virtuoso display, especially in Act II, yet I left the theatre feeling in some way disappointed and I wasn't sure why. The next evening I saw Patricia Ruanne and Jay Jolley, and my disappointment of the previous evening was quickly explained. This second evening I saw the ballet as it should be. The two Principals were a part of the whole work, giving a totally convincing performance, telling the

tragic and moving story through beautiful dance charged with emotion. I left the theatre feeling elated and drained but realizing I had learnt something important about performing.

About a year later during my first season with the Royal Ballet I was given the opportunity to dance the Florestan *pas de trois* in the third act of *Sleeping Beauty*. This was my very first solo with the Company and I can still remember the thrill of seeing the two girls who were dancing with me go off stage leaving just me in the middle on my own. I remember having time to think that this was my big chance and I had better not mess it up. I took off for the first jump and landed rather unsteadily, realized what I was doing and pulled myself together for the rest of the dance. I can't remember if I finished it well, but that first step on my own I'll never forget.

The third event happened on the night of the première of David Bintley's ballet *Galanteries,* in which I had my first choreographed solo. The solo was a piece of pure classical dance, neat clean footwork, *placement*, *port de bras* and *epaulement*, all of which Brian Shaw, then the company teacher, tried to instill in us during his classes. Immediately after the performance Brian came backstage to congratulate me and told me how much it had meant to him to see me putting his teaching into practice on the stage. To receive praise from someone you really respect can make it all worthwhile.

JACK WYNGAARD

LONDON CITY BALLET

M Y INTRODUCTION to ballet is quite bizarre! At the age of sixteen I was at a disco in Cape Town when someone told me I should go to jazz classes. I successfully auditioned for a part in *Showboat* and decided I would like to continue working in the theatre. I performed in several operas, including Harlequin in *Don Pasquale* and a doll in *The Tales of Hoffmann*. This experience developed my love of opera, my favourite composer being Verdi.

The Tales of Hoffmann was choreographed by Veronica Paeper, who was Resident Choreographer of the CAPAB Ballet. She told me that extras were needed for the company's production of *Romeo and Juliet*, so I carried a spear! I used to sit by the door watching the company doing class and David Poole, the Director at that time, asked me to do classes at the school. I got a bursary straightaway to join the school – I was then eighteen. It is a three-year course but after only a year and a half I was offered a place in the company and immediately danced the Bluebird in *Sleeping Beauty*. After that, things got better and better and I also created a few roles, including Mercury in *Orpheus in the Underworld*.

I was with CAPAB for five years and always wore costumes which had been worn by Harold King, although I didn't know who he was! One day I saw in the papers that he was coming to Cape Town for a holiday, so I wrote and invited him to a performance. He offered me a job and I joined London City Ballet in 1986. My first impression when I came to England was that it was just like home – I loved London.

Dancers don't have much spare time for hobbies – I collect videos of old musicals. I enjoy hang-gliding, but that's a forbidden sport these days! I also used to do some ice-skating before I started dancing.

Although I returned to CAPAB for a season, when I danced in *Le Spectre de la Rose*, *Les Patineurs* and the solo from *Le Corsaire*, I want to stay in London – this is my home now.

MIYAKO YOSHIDA

THE BIRMINGHAM ROYAL BALLET

From a very early age I enjoyed sport and being active. I remember seeing my friends dancing and was impressed by their beautiful costumes. I eventually persuaded my mother to allow me to go to ballet classes when I was nine. Right from the beginning I found them challenging – our teacher always made the class difficult – but at the same time it was something which I really enjoyed.

Since joining the company, the hard work has continued – long rehearsals, frequent travel and dancing on different stages – but the thrill of the actual performance, the excitement of being on stage, makes up for everything.

Dancers always suffer injuries and it's taking me a long time to learn how to work my own body. Each person is different and it is important to know your own body and its limitations. Before this season I suffered a back injury which meant I couldn't dance for eight months, and I found it very hard. However, I used the time to develop other interests – including reading, listening to music, watching films – and I think it is important to do this in order to develop your own personality.

Above all, I think I'm extremely fortunate that dancing, which is something I love so much, is also my job.

INDEX

PICTURE CREDITS